Broken Vessel

Broken Vessel

by

Kitty

ISBN: 1-5872-1825-9

This book is printed on acid free paper.

1stBooks - rev. 07/25/02

About the Book

The purpose of this three-part manuscript is to encourage others like myself to believe that God is with them and working all things out to His glory and their good. Beginning by describing my life in a detailed autobiographical section. In this section I relate the circumstances surrounding my pregnancies and children's births; my relationship with an abusive husband, and what followed after his death, a tragic accident and a miraculous recovery; the loss of my fiancée to an untimely death; and my experience as a foster parent. The second part is an exhortation to always walk in love, no matter what; to crucify the flesh and walk in the power of the Holy Spirit. I challenge the Church to wake up and do her job, for a dying world is waiting in need. The final part is a series of poems written by me, which describe my walk and relationship with my Heavenly Father.

"INTRODUCTION"

The reason for this book is four-fold and above all is for the glory of my Lord, Savior and soon coming King. Of which all my expressions of love and gratitude is owed to Him alone, and to no other.

The second reason is that God's hand is upon it, my life and the reason and cause for me to write it at this time.

Third, is that there are many Kitty's [male and female], out there right now who are reading this book, needing to know they like I, are never alone in the struggles of this life. God will use every situation in our lives, proving it to be to His good and glory. We must not forget how very important we are to Him, no matter what it is that we go through it is all nothing compared to the glory we will share with our Lord on that day of great celebration.

Fourth, is of God's reminder to me of His goodness towards me, His faithfulness with me, the grace and mercy poured out upon me through it all, and daily I am reminded of His abounding "Love", within me.

The title chosen for a favorite scripture of mine, [Luke 7:37-50] tells the story of a woman that was an uninvited guest, who only had eyes sat upon her Lord Jesus, and He alone. It mattered not that she was not invited or wanted she came in and remained at the feet of her dear Lord. Anointing his feet with the expensive perfumed oil, contained within an alabaster jar. She began to weep as she bathed his feet with her tears and to wipe them dry with her hair.

She did not move, it mattered not to her of her surroundings or whose eyes were upon her, she lovingly remained and bowed at His feet. Pouring out her self, her love offering out upon her Savior, as others only looked on to judge her.

In this scripture God began to reveal many truths to me as I read His word yet one truth remained to stand out, it is this:

> "The vessels use, like this alabaster jar
> is of no use, unless it is broken open, so

> that it's true worth contained within can
> then be poured out."

We, God showed me are these jars, the containers, worthless unless we too are broken open so that our true worth contained within us, [the Holy Spirit], can then be poured out from us so that "He", may be made known.

I am a broken vessel of God's choice and will for my life, and do remain at the feet of Jesus. Like this woman I have no concerns of my surroundings, or do I care of the unlooking eyes, or their perception of me. I like this woman know of the forgiveness of Jesus. I too will to remain at the feet of "Him", to submit all until the "Potter", is finished with this lump of clay.

Therefore Jesus says in [Luke 7:47], her sins which were many have been forgiven; hence she has shown great love. But the one to whom little is forgiven loves little. Then Jesus said to this woman, "Your sins are forgiven." But those who were at the table sitting around with Jesus began to say among themselves, who is this who even forgives sins? Then Jesus said to the woman, "Your faith has saved you; go in peace."

Here we see love and forgiveness from Jesus, even after He forgave, others remained to hold her sins not only against her but also questioned Jesus on His forgiveness. Are we remaining to be as these men today? If we are forgiven as this woman why do people put themselves above Christ and His blood and hold us in a position of less?

We must remember it is God's grace through faith that saves us, not our act of doing anything for Him. Least of all not us trying to do good or to be good. It is nothing within us that we come to this place.

The faith this woman showed by her actions was honored by God. We must remove ourselves from the position that these men took at the table, and only remember this, [it is not about you or I, or anything we have done or could ever do, it is all about Jesus and what He has already done for us, it is all complete and contained in and upon the cross.]

Also we must not continue to think so highly of ourselves, and to even give our opinion of another. Who are we? After all we are suppose to be dead aren't we? It is Christ who now lives in and through us. God is no longer as in the days of old carried around in a "Tabernacle", it is now us, you and I, the "Body of Christ", here on earth that now house this loving, awesome, powerful presence. We are now His resting place. [I Corinthians 6:19-20] "Or do you not know that your body is the temple of the Holy Spirit who is "in" you, whom you have from God, and you are not your own? For you were bought at a price; therefore glorify God in your body and in your spirit, which are God's."

We are God's house! No different today than as then, God wants the same, our love, honor, respect and most of all our obedience. He desires fellowship with us, He made us, chose us, and now wants us to return to Him, trusting in all His ways. No matter what our situation or whose eyes are upon us, to come in loving trust and obedience as did the woman in scripture. God honored her faith and He will ours too, if we come.

Here I recall a passage of scripture which is rich in it's content, it is in [Psalm 118:8], "It is better to take refuge in the Lord, than to put your trust in man."

Here God tells us to take refuge in the Lord. The word refuge is powerful and here implies, [shelter or protection from danger or distress, a safe place.]

Under His refuge I have remained, and you will see as the pages pass that this scripture has held me in that safe place for many years. As I wrote I remembered how it felt to not be able to breathe at times, at others to be reminded of the ongoing tears that fell sometimes daily. I would feel as though I would drown in them, the pain so great it would engulf me. I only wanted out! Yet I was not going anywhere, for my life was to be tried.

Oh but God! Taking His word and proving it true to me, would come along side saying to me. "Hold on to me, believe in me, trust only I, don't look to man for the answers nor the shelter from your trials, I alone will pull you up and out!" The faithfulness I received from Him was so tender, I hung on to His every word, for it was all I had. No matter what my circumstances looked like, I'm reminded in His word to neither go by sight nor feelings, and I would soon find out why! They both will pull you down faster than any tidal wave, to there drown you in the misery of self.

For God knew I had seen it all and had felt it all, but taught me to hold on to His word above it all. All proving to be for my good, the trials great teachers, at times as I sat at the desk of life I learned many truths. Once in the middle of a trial I cried out, "Oh God have I graduated yet?" I quickly assured Him I was only kidding, and in return He assured me that He already knew!

I will tell of the trials of my life in the times of which they came to me, and will follow through the years as they continued to rain upon me. All along my umbrella was up sheltering me from the rain, I would run and take refuge in my Lord until the storm passed. I stayed close to my Father, for there was always another storm brewing around the corner of my life.

At the end I will enter some Songs and Poems, God has used me to bring forth. I now know there is much that God wants to share with us, wanting us to know Him. Always know as you read this book on parts of my life, I take nothing for myself except the healing that was given me of God. It is all for Him, the one who sits upon the throne. Worthy is the Lamb that sits there and came to take away the sins of the world.

Realizing to be as Christ is to be a broken vessel before God. For to be this broken vessel it is in that breaking that then we may be made whole, to the likeness of His Son Christ Jesus! Being broken will lead us all into that life of Holiness, Purity, Love. For Love is the light that needs to shine.

Many of us need to become that light as Christ was to the world around us. For lives are being affected all around us, for the good and the bad, it all depends what we are projecting forth.

My life in as well as out of the church has proven one does not have to be of another color to be asked to sit to the back of the bus. God showed me it has been like this since the days of this women in [Luke 7:37-50], and it hasn't changed today. It in itself portrays an act of superiority on ones behalf towards another.

To be looked upon in disgust, to be told to sit down and where, how to respond to a situation, to be ignored, left out, spit upon, laughed at. To be made lower than others, told you don't fit in, or to be the cause of another's faults, to be talked about, or slandered, and all for what? So one can feel better than! Better than what? We have done nothing than to have lowered ourselves to the very depths of God's enemy, can't we see this is what the devil did to Jesus! Then why in the world have we done it to one another?

For the beam has been hanging out of our own eye the entire time we have been trying to get the speck from our brothers eye. Such a foolish waste of time on our part! For no one has made us judge and jury but ourselves, and the sentence is about to be passed! Why would we want to even be here?

"Judge not, and you shall not be judged. Condemn not, and you shall not be condemned. Forgive, and you shall be forgiven. Give, and it will be given to you: good measure, pressed down, shaken together, and running over will be put into your bosom. For with the same measure that you use, it will be measured back to you." [Luke 6:37-38] This scripture is not on giving money!

This scripture clearly is on compassion, forgiving and our mercy towards others, we will reap what we sow! His mercy to you and I is the example set down for us to extend to others. Not to judge others, for this puts us in a dangerous place.

But love your enemies, do good, and lend, expecting nothing in return. Your reward will be great, and you will be children of the Most High; for he is kind to the ungrateful and the wicked. Be merciful, just as your Father is merciful. [Luke 6:35) We are made in His Image! The image is that of Spirit, we do as He wills, to become the image of Him. Even to love those that hurt us, even our enemies, for even God is kind to the ungrateful and the wicked, being merciful! As He continues to be with you and I, we are called to no less.

We will know if we are in His image by the fruit we bear towards others. See even ones in the church say they serve God, maybe so! But it has been the god of self! They have made themselves a god, by placing themselves not only above people but above God. For even God is compassionate, as we should be.

No, one does not have to be told to sit to the back of the bus to be treated wrongly. Whether then or now it leaves a bad taste in the mouth of God, and we best begin to remove ourselves from each others gaze, thought, or hands for it is a dangerous place to be for a child of God.

See this is an age old game played by satan since creation. But we as the Body of Christ need not play along any longer, for he is a loser, church! Why would we want to be a part of the losing team? Read the back of the book church! We win!

And I am here to tell you satan is defeated!

> "But they have conquered him by the blood of the Lamb, and by the word of their testimony." [Revelation 12:11]

The blood supplied by Jesus and the testimony supplied by us, as is mine between these pages as we continue. Church! He lost then and he will only now continue to keep losing. We must not allow ourselves to be continually deceived by a defeated foe.

You see Jesus had a job to do when He came here, and He is finished! We too have a job to do church, and we are far from being finished, there is still much for us to do. It was finished when the final blow to satan came when the Lamb of God, Jesus, shed His blood upon the cross for you and I. For our sins that kept us separated from God our Father. Christ alone brings this victory, yet we too now must stand up and let everyone know what He has done for us in the battles of our own lives.

Until that day, let us, "Submit to God, Resist the devil, and he will flee from us." [James 4:7] This is God's word, He said it, not us. Therefore it is the truth, because He can not lie. We must now believe Him.

Submit means to "GIVE UP", "YIELD" to the authority, power or will of another, this is what we are told to do towards God. To "RESIST", means to work or strive against, to "OPPOSE", any force that tends to hinder motion, to be set against or to "FIGHT", we must do this towards satan. First we submit to God, do not ever believe satan will leave you alone if you are not submitted or yielded first. Then God tells us to resist him, then he will flee from us. It is just not saying the scripture, we must act upon God's word. Faith without works on our part is dead, this walk we are called into is action upon God's word.

After we submit, then we resist, then he will flee. Flee means more than just to go away, it entails to run away from, to remove swiftly from any danger! This scripture holds power for us, for satan to flee from us means he is moving fast from us cause we can cause him danger when and if we are submitted to God.

Let us not only read the word but be doers of it also. Not to be used of the enemy to be against one another. For in doing so we only prove who we are serving! See, satan comes to deceive, and by the looks of it he has done it to many of us. The word also tells us that "if", it could be in the last days even the very elect would be deceived. We better wake up church! Look around us! What has been dished out to us? And why have we been eating it?

Let us also not portray the act of superiority towards one another any longer, especially since we know who it is coming from. It has only brought division amongst the brethren, we are not suppose to be the accuser of the brethren are we? Satan is! We should not play along with him any longer, it is a dangerous ground to be found on. Amen! Let us not be caught in that dangerous place by God, and become a bad taste in His mouth. Let us yield to God our Father, our authority over our lives, giving in to His power and will. To strive against the devil, pressing in to oppose the force that tends to hinder our motion forward.

We must be set against our enemy as we are told and fight with the ammunition supplied us in the Blood, the Word and in our Testimony.

To not forget how important it is how we treat each other, for in the measure we give forth is the measure we will receive. (Luke 6:36-38) Be merciful, just as He! God is clearly telling us here it is a quality birthed in us for giving of ourselves one to another. We are not only to be this way to those in the realm of our thinking! Our compassion must be that of Christ. The amount we measure out will be returned unto us. This is not if we feel like it, it is a way of life for us, just as well as it was for Christ.

To love your neighbor as your self, to do unto others as we would want done unto us, to forgive so that we might be forgiven, loving even our enemies. Being above someone only separates us from the hand of God! Submitting to Him and His Will, brings us to Him! That's exactly where you want to be, with God. By doing the other we are only headed for trouble spiritually and physically.

As we walk this walk down here, all may seem senseless and useless for us. Oh, but God has a bigger picture, from the beginning to the end. The picture we perceive with our natural eye is not how God sees it, remember we walk by faith and not by sight. No eye has seen the true things of God. Yet!

Only the image we are to be cast into can bring us there, as a whole, as we were created to be, now the Body of Christ. We were made in His image! Not only in Spirit, but to do all in the Spirit.

My life, your life, all for a reason. No matter what it looks like or feels like. We must only do as God tells us and as Jesus did before us. No matter the cost to us, it will be worth it in the end. All for Him, our loving Father that continues to call us all home.

Many as you read will be able to relate to my life in many areas, others it will be hard for you to even perceive. Yet as you read only look between the lines of my life and see "Him", amidst it all. He is the reason for it all, and all glory is due Him.

All of my trials are not contained here, for only what He wants to go forth now is what I will bring forth. For the ones He knows would be holding this book would be the ones He cares to take higher, to a place only in Him. We can only get there by going through what we have gone through here, as our example before us did.

To suffer the hardships of Christ as a good soldier, (2nd Timothy 2:3)

No difference, we now the Body of Christ have this right of passage also.

Beloved, do not be surprised at the fiery ordeals or trials among you, which come upon you for "your testing" as though some strange thing were happening to you; but to the degree that you "share the sufferings of Christ", keep on rejoicing; so that also at the revelation of His glory, you may rejoice with exultation.

All God's will, as was when Christ died for us and paid for our sins, this act restored us to have relationship with our heavenly Father. Now we must stand and not let satan reclaim ground, we must occupy. Occupy means to take, and hold possession of, to hold on to the ground won through the death of Christ! It was not for nothing that He came here and gave His life for you and I. It was for us, we now the purposed "Bride".

Yet He is coming for a Bride without spot or wrinkle, we are now being made ready for that day. Many say we could be out of here any day, another lie from satan. That way we can stay comfortable, complacent and off guard! Satan wants none of us to be prepared, he wants us without oil in our lamps.

For if we think God did all that He did for all of this! No way! The shape the Body of Christ is in, we as the church are greatly mistaken.

We the Bride are in sad shape, spiritually we are not dressed! We are limping towards the isle with one shoe on, our dress isn't zipped up, our hair is un-kept, and we've lost sight of our first love!

Church we are not ready! We have been lulled to sleep! We best wake up!

"Shall we begin"

I give you a new commandment
that you love one another.
Just as I Jesus have loved you
you also should love one
another. By this everyone will
know that you are my disciples
"if" you have love for one
another.

John 13:34-35

"EMPTY CRADLE"

As a child grows within you, it not only grows at a high speed but then so does the mother. With my twenty-seven pounds gained, all doctors visits kept, vitamins taken, rest until noon on some days. All the right foods eaten, and now nine months behind me. I was now ready!

Or so I thought until that day arrived, it was a few days before the holidays, the tree up, presents wrapped I had just finished up with some laundry and was entering the kitchen to fix me a bite to eat. When a huge sharp cramp came across my lower abdomen. I stood still bent over as I held on to the counter. It was all I could do to make it down the hall-way to the bedroom, as I laid across the bed the pain begins to overwhelm my entire body.

Not having a baby before I had no idea what to expect, and nothing I had read could prepare me for how I felt or what was about to happen to me. The contractions now doubling me over, curled up on my bed I reach for the phone calling the hospital. They inform me that my Doctor is at a Christmas party and couldn't be disturbed unless it was an emergency, I was told to time my contractions and come in only when they were three minutes apart. I called a friend and she came over and sat with me as she timed by contractions, she told me, it looks like you are already to three minutes apart. We headed for the hospital, upon my arrival I could tell the nurse that greeted me was less than happy. It was late, quiet, and all her patients were asleep, the entire Hospital staff was at the Christmas party at the Elks Lodge. Adding to the nurses discomfort was me about to give birth, what a time to have a baby was written all over her face, she didn't know that I wasn't doing all that well either, nor was I going to stay home and be a brave pioneer woman and have this baby at home.

She now has me sit in a wheel-chair and takes me to the Labor Room, has me undress so she can check and see how far I've dilated, then letting me know I can put my clothes back on. She informs me that I have not even made it to the half point, to put my clothes back on that I could go home. I laid there staring at the ceiling still feeling the pain as it filled my body. She leaves, I try and sit up to re-position myself, the cramps now moving from my back to my lower stomach. The pain now begins to arch my back taking me to a sitting position, I reach for the buzzer to ring for the nurse. It takes a while for her to return, when she does I ask her to check me again. She can tell that I'm scared and tells me this being my first baby it was false labor, that I was getting all worked up for nothing. Just go home and get some rest, and the Doctor could see me in his office in the morning. She now leaves again, I lay there alone looking up at the clock on the wall up in front of me. The room freezing, it is beyond quiet, the cramps will not stop, and my body is shaking.

I now become filled with pain of enormous strength, it is now stronger and coming with intense pressure. I close my eyes to try and not focus too much on the pain that was now unbearable. The clock upon the wall seems to be getting larger as the time passes, the second hand going slower and slower.

I lay there helpless on a tiny table half the length of me with a sheet of paper draped over me. My mouth dry from breathing hard, my lips swollen and cracked, I can't even sit up, let alone get up. I know I can't leave, remaining to stare at the clock, I now am shivering with cold chills bringing goose bumps to my skin.

I can't believe the joy of bringing a new life into the world would be so alone, the feeling I couldn't escape as I laid helpless with no one at my side. It crushed my very sense of all that I looked forward to as I grew up as a little girl, thoughts swirled through my head as I laid there trying my hardest to cope with it all.

I cry out as a pain lifts me almost off the table, I reach for the buzzer again to call for the nurse. Gripping the sides of the table I try and sit up, the pain consuming my back. The next pain brings me to tears, with my water breaking and going everywhere, I can feel the baby coming out. I am afraid to push, for if I do I know the baby would come. I can feel it's head pressing on me and pushing itself free to come out. At this time the nurse comes in.

The nurse begins to yell at me, "what are you doing"? I'm crying and answer, "I told you I was going to have this baby." She reaches towards the paper sheet across my legs and takes it off, "No, she yells now you can't have this baby now," as she sees the baby's head is coming out, she leans over and holds my legs shut. My body now trembling all over, I can't stop it. The room is freezing cold, the back of my legs are beginning to cramp up on me. I think she is going to help me, only to see her walk out the door again. I try to slow my breathing so not to be too scared, as I now am left alone again. I feel as though I'm going to pass out, I tell myself to calm down, to stop crying, it will all be over with soon. I begin to feel as though I'm going to pass out, feeling dizzy, sick and extremely cold. The pain continuing to travel from my back to the lower stomach area, it all continues to come in un-controllable fear and disbelief.

The door opens. It is my doctor and many others following him up to my bedside. I lay back and now cry, he assures me it will be alright. They proceed to wheel me into the delivery room, as I lay there I know I could take no more, exhausted, the sounds around me becoming muffled, the people blurry. I continue to push, it is extremely bright under the lights, everyone is slowly fading away.

It is over, the baby is here. No one is saying a word, a mask is put over my face, I feel sick. I don't hear any crying! A voice comes to my ear and tells me, it was a boy Kitty, but he is dead! I hear it over and over in my head as I pass out.

The next thing I am aware of is I wake up in a bed in the maternity ward, next to a woman nursing her baby. Family is gathered at her side with sighs of joy, words of love and presents galore. I turn my head towards the window, as I stare out I ask the nurse that walked in to pull the curtain between ours beds. The ache in me was one of unbearable grief, even the smell of the newborn baby was filling the room with a sweetness that filled my nostrils. A nurse walks in and says the doctor is coming to make his rounds all family and friends had to leave. Everything in me wanted to get up and leave with them, but I was still weak and drifted back off to sleep.

My doctor comes in and realizes they made a mistake and had put me in the wrong room, papers were flying everywhere and he was asking for the nurse on duty. How did she get in here, look at her chart. The girl in the bed next to me starts to cry, she gets up and comes over to hug my neck, asking if I wanted to hold her baby.

My doctor has me moved that second to a room alone, he tells me if my husband gets home from work that I could go home. My husband did come home to the news of what happened, he didn't talk about it then or ever to me. The drive home was quiet, pulling into the drive of our home the hound dogs were out to greet us. I went in, he carried in my belongings with him. I walked to the bedroom passing the huge picture window in the living room that gave a beautiful view of the river out back. It felt as though I had been gone a long time instead of only two days. As I reached the bedroom I found it emptied of all my baby things.

I went out side to find my husband and ask where all the things had gone? Choking back my tears I ask! He tells me I didn't think you'd be wanting to be bothered with any of it. The bear too, I ask? What bear he asks? I cry as I tell him, the one my parents bought for the baby, that has sat in the cradle for these past nine months. Why do you want it now he asks? Oh just to hold it, smell it, run my fingers through the blue satin ribbon tied around its neck, I answer!

He continues to water without an answer, I can feel the coldness come off him like the winters night air, both chilling. I again try and bring up the baby, as I held on to the tie that loosely was wrapped around the robe I had on. What happened? When was his funeral? Talk to me! He just stares at me. I felt as though I was talking about something that had nothing to do with me, as if I was trapped in a nightmare.

I went inside to lay down and rest, only to find my mind retracing the moments of the days before. I did get my bear, of which I found comfort in, making me realize it wasn't really a bad dream after all. As I held something of the memory in my hands, it soothed my mind for the time I held on to it. The loss my arms felt was at times painful, yet the girl in the Hospital had me over for lunch and we became buddies, she letting me help her with her baby, also a boy.

There was a time I drove through the cemetery looking for the headstone of my son, yet it was never to be found by me. I thought how sad, will he ever be thought of at all by anyone? I left that day never to return to ask anymore questions of the man tending to the grounds, he could see the pain on my face the hurt in my unanswered questions. So I drove away, as I left the entrance I prayed.

Lord, I know you have my son, he is with you. In my memory I will carve a headstone for him and it will read.

Shawn Lee, born December 22, 1969: died December 22, 1969. The much loved and wanted son of Kitty, now safe in the arms of Jesus.

No birth certificate, no death certificate, no one talks to me of it. I begin to think it was not all real, especially now since I had found no marked grave sight, nor could the man at the cemetery help me. What had they done with him?

Yet my body did not lie, it had all the signs, within too it was apparent. The tears that I cried alone for my son were real, warm as they fell against the silence of the night. My pillow drenched with the memory each morning brought back to me as I laid there tightly holding my bear that somehow now brought me some comfort. My bear seemed also to have the markings of such loss written across his face, we were in this together. For my arms held the pain within that no one could console.

To lose a son, your only son, it was a loss that I held dear to me then and now. In a basket next to my bed is the bear along with other stuffed animals, reminding me daily of the time we will be together, it brings a smile to my face. The knowing within me holds my arms to ever hold dear the time I will hold my son. Till then I know he is in the best of hands with my Father.

"WHAT'S HER NAME I ASK?"

The time passed, it now repeated itself, I again am wearing maternity clothes. My due date came and went, my doctor has me in for tests to see if there are any complications. They find the baby is turned wrong, laying sideways across width wise from one of my sides to the other. The baby wrapped in the cord, and apparently when it had tried to turn it got caught, the cord cramped off, the baby now in distress. My doctor has me go home to pack a overnight bag and return for an emergency c-section in the morning.

I drive home in disbelief, my face red from crying I go in the house. I go to the bedroom to pack, my husband walks in asks what are you doing? I explain to him what the doctor told me, I start crying. He glares at me and states, isn't there anything you can do right? I am hurt, but swallow back my tears to finish packing. I stand in silence, I don't want to get upset and hurt the baby any worse.

I arrive at the hospital, they are waiting for me, we do paper work, prep me for surgery, and finish up with hooking me up to I.V.s. They finish, my doctor comes in and checks me, explains the surgery to me, and leaves. I can rest now and they will wake me in a few hours to take me in to the operating room. Everyone leaves, lights turned down low, side rails pulled up, I lay there in the stillness of it all. Rubbing my belly I think this will be the last time I see you so big, in the morning it will be no more, and instead I will be holding my angel, a tiny new life, my baby.

The hours pass fast, it is time, I'm helped over to another bed and then wheeled down to surgery. The lights are bright as they position me under them in the surgery room. The moment was here, it was all scary to me, it made me feel out of sorts, and again scared.

It seemed like it took no time until they were done. The waiting was over they announce it is a girl! The room again becomes quiet, they hurry the baby off to an isolette. She is not breathing, they begin to work on her and hook her up to wires and oxygen. She is having problems, I turn my head to not look. Oh God! I cry out. No! Not again! Again I'm put out.

Later I awake in my hospital room, the nurse putting another blanket on me. Another woman from medical records asking if I'm awake enough to do some paper work, she is holding a clip board and states, female, weight 5lbs. 15oz., 20in. long, name Kathleen. I stop her! Her name isn't Kathleen I say, her name is Mariah. The woman states that is what your husband filled out in the office for us, for the birth certificate. At that he walks in, and I tell them I won't sign the birth certificate to her name being that.

My doctor now walks in, he explains to me that the baby is in great danger, they have called for an air ambulance to come and fly her out to L.A. He asks me if I'd like to see her before they take her away! They can roll her up to my door as they pass by, for the isolette won't fit through the door and because of my surgery they won't allow me to get up. Yes I tell him, but please I really want to get up and go to her.

He walks to the door and leaves to finish the transfer papers on her. At that moment she is wheeled up to my door. I could hardly take it, the pain I felt was inescapable. I wanted to touch her, hold her so bad. Her lifeless tiny body laying helplessly in that bed of glass, all hooked up to wires. Her innocent little body motionless, except for her chest grasping for air, as it sunk in and collapsed with each breath she took. Her legs the size of my baby finger, her color was red, and her hair so light it was transparent. Only for a second she was before me in that door way, yet my mind captured a picture in my memory, for me to hold on to till God allowed her to come home to me. I had to hold on, be strong for my daughter, she was weak, I too could not be.

I fell asleep crying, the priest from our local parish came in woke me to let me know she had gotten off alright. That he blessed her and baptized her in case of death. I start to fall apart now, crying with such pain within me, I tell him she didn't have a name, I didn't get to name her. He tells me everything is just fine. I named her he tells me. "What's her name, I ask?" He says to me he took my first baby's name and feminized it. Her name is Shawna Leann. Oh! I tell him thank you, it is beautiful and perfect. Crying still he hugs my shoulder and says to me, it will be fine, you hang in there and trust God.

My stay this time was longer in the hospital. I had to recover from the c-section, getting up each day to walk, and get stronger. Yet my arms were again empty, as was my hospital room from flowers or congratulations. I would think to myself as I healed, about my baby so far away from me. Were the nurses holding her? Were they taking good care of her? Did they think she was as pretty and special, as I did?

Weeks came and went, everyday I waited for news of her progress, waited for her to be well enough to make the long trip home. For she had to be on assistance for breathing, still weak, and she had been losing weight. The day did come, I could hardly contain myself, my arms were hurting just to hold her.

Yet my husband wouldn't allow me to go with him to pick her up from the Hospital, he was going to take his sister. Please I cried at the door, I begged him as he walked out, please I'll just sit in the car till we get there and get her and we can drive home. No! He yelled as he walked out and shut the door.

I slumped against the door and slid down to a laying position, I layed there weak from the hurt and wept for some time. The day was long as I waited for her to come home, I felt horrible to what she had to come home to. I try and busy myself, I rearrange her clothes in the dressing table my parents had bought for my first baby. The same cradle sits in the corner next to my side of the bed, a night light that dimly shadows the room with soft hues of pink. A white delicate lace blanket drapes over the edge of the cradle. I sit and look at it all for it seems like hours. It all calms me though, she'll be home soon, it won't be long, I say to myself. For there was no one for me to talk to about it all. I walked through the house checking, just to make sure it was all clean and ready for her.

Night had sat in, it was extremely quiet now, I fix me something to eat, and sit on the sofa. The door opens, my sister-in-law walks in with my baby in her arms. I reach for her, take her little body into my arms and begin to unwrap her.

I take her still tiny finger in my hand and raise it to my lips and kiss it, saying you are beautiful. I do so love you, and I am glad your home.

She would as the years pass get caught between the cross fire between her father and I. She would have to grow up strong to live with the things that were about to be placed before her innocent little life.

"HER NAME IS TRINITY"

Some eight years later, and many painful times of ugliness in between. I now find myself wearing maternity clothes again. Due to all my previous problems with my pregnancies my doctor set a date for me to have a scheduled c-section. It would be the day after the fourth of July.

I go in the evening of the fourth, and they do all the needed paper work, prep me for surgery in the early morning. After they were all done with me I layed in the hospital bed listening to the fireworks going off out side. Thinking to myself all the yummy foods prepared would have to wait for me next year. The fried chicken, potato salad, the chocolate flag cake with whip cream frosting, would not be putting extra pounds on me just yet, I sure did think about it though! Now I just was waiting for the morning, for my "firecracker baby", to arrive.

I ask my girlfriend to go buy a baby doll for Shawna and wrap it up in one of the hospital receiving blankets, and to give it to her when I deliver. I didn't want her to feel left out, cause she and I had become a pair all those years by ourselves. She had become my ear, my pillow to cry on, and hugs at night, we were very close and even being in there away from her made me feel horrible.

The long familiar trip begins again down the corridor of the hospital, to be wheeled into the operating room. There I'm given a shot in my lower back to numb me from my upper tummy to the tips of my toes, I feel nothing! They begin the surgery, the room is cold, the smell is sterile and the lights are even brighter it seems this time. It is over, they tell me "Kitty, it's a girl!" Of which I'm happy for, another precious daughter a gift of God. A baby girl, how sweet, Shawna will have a baby sister. My husband wouldn't share in my delight, for he wanted a son. But I signed to get my tubes tied that day as well, no more baby's for me, my days of that adventure were over I thought.

They are scrambling in the room about me, there is another problem with this baby as well, she stops breathing! They take her to the side away from my view. I am in shock, this baby too? No Lord! Please help her live!

They attempt to put me out again, I resist this time. I hear them talking all around me, they say clean her up and get her out of here to a recovery room. I am told as they wheel me out this baby too will be air lifted out, but not to L.A., for this baby wouldn't make it that far. She will go to Las Vegas instead, it is closer. A specialist is called in from San Diego to meet them there. She is immediately taken away and prepared to leave. I will not get to see her, or hold this baby either.

They can't risk any time, on the way the air-lock breaks down and I'm told she is given mouth to mouth. I thought as I layed there in that bed, well Kitty three strikes and your out. The medical staff arrives again, to finish up the paper work for there records.

I am asked her name. I tell them "her name is Trinity", Trinity Lanae. The nurse states to me, what a beautiful name, I bet your daughter is as pretty as her name. I smile and say, choking back the tears, yes she is! I turn my head as they all walk out and sob. I hold on to the hope that rises up in me, I only have a promise from God, and I hold on to it.

I again go home empty handed, the cradle waits again in her room for her to come home. Her room is done in yellow gingham checks, it is delightfully bright and pretty as she will be, I think to myself as I stood in the door way looking around. She will love it.!

I'm healing quicker from the surgery than the last, maybe because it's summer out and the warmth gives me energy. I just wait till she is better to come home and be with her sister and I. We do get the call that she can come home, yet I'm told I can't go with him again to get this baby either! This time he takes my sister with him. I am saddened by it all, yet Shawna is good company for me, we will wait together.

I walk to the door of the baby's room, stopping to look around. I go in and sit in the rocker and stare out the window. I wait again for my arms to be filled. But as I sat there my other memories filled my mind. I slump in the rocker holding my face in my hands, sobbing from it all. Now this memory too, tucked in with the rest.

Later that day they pull up, I go out to meet them, camera in hand. She is carried in by my sister, I too reach for this baby. I take her in my arms and we walk inside. I sit in the living area, and unwrap her also. She seems even smaller than Shawna was. Shawna comes over, I give her baby sister to her to hold on the sofa, she is soft and sweet with her.

She wants to hold her all the time as the days follow, I tell her wait for her to wake up first. She'd run in to get me after awhile and say she's awake! I'd laugh and tell her, well she wouldn't be if you would stop waking her up. We would laugh, and she would soon find out that when the baby was asleep that was our time together.

As the years past they became buddies, Shawna with her big blue eyes and blonde hair, and Trinity with her huge almond shaped brown eyes and honey colored hair. So different in looks, yet sisters at heart. I was proud to be their mama!

I came to realize I was truly blessed to have them, and though the pain was tremendous that I would have to eventually bear. It was worth all to me, to have them by my side. God knew all along what He was doing!

"A LONELY MAN"

My husband was a very abusive man, not only to me but to many others. His life seemed to me and others as being full, happy and having everything. The appearance of was important to him, he had all the materialistic prizes, including me, as many joked over the years. I had just become another trophy to sit on his shelf. At times it would seem as if things would get better, then without notice his world seemed to go hay-wire. One never knew what to expect, yet I always wanted to believe in him and to expect the best.

He not only physically abused me, but verbally and mentally as well. He through the years progressed, trying to strangle me, drown me, suffocate me, shoot me, and to beat me as a man. Drop kicking me to the floor many times, my eyes had been blackened, my jaw swollen, welts and bruises up and down my body, he left no stone unturned.

He would tear up little pieces of papers, dating them and hide them around the house under legs of furniture. Just to see if I had cleaned and had moved the furniture that day to vacuum. Everyday was spring cleaning to him. Other times he moved the refrigerator out from the wall in the kitchen to see if I had cleaned the dust off the coils. If any dust remained I wore it across my face. The laundry had to be done at all times, he would not allow any dirty clothes in the hamper. His clothes had to be ironed and alternated every week, front to back, so he would not repeat wearing the same clothes.

The table had to be set just right, the salt and pepper within his reach, and the bread and butter too. If anything was wrong according to him, he would throw it all to the floor with one sweep of his hand, and of course I got to pick it all up.

He had many women, behind my back as well as many in front of me, some in our own home, he didn't care. He reminded me everyday if I didn't like it I could leave, but I was not taking the girls. So I stayed, I was not going anywhere without them, and he knew it. He would tell me, you don't like it here leave, there's the door. Women were a dime a dozen to him, he could find one off the street to replace me, and be a mom to my girls. So I stayed. I knew his threats were not idle, I had seen too many times him carry out his word, hurting many.

I did the best I could to keep the peace, yet nothing made him happy. Even our two beautiful daughters were not enough to keep him home. Or to realize he had all he ever needed here with us. It was sad to watch him over the years, to be so busy, yet never to accomplish a thing. It was all wasted time and effort on his part. So lonely a man and yet it was all before him the entire time, such gifts from God put into his lap. But blind to it all, I would cry many a night and pray for it all to get better, I hated all that he was heading towards.

He sold drugs out of our home, we had people at all hours coming to our house, many of high reputation around town. When Shawna was a child she learned to count as she bagged reds, and cross tops on our den floor at home. I knew he was baiting me with many things that he did, wanting a reaction from me so we could fight and he could get me to leave or give him reason to leave. Such a game it had all became to him over the years, his entire life was quickly running out before his very eyes.

Often he pretended to go to work sitting outside and watching me through the windows, later coming in laughing and saying you better watch your back, you just never know who could be watching you. I wasn't allowed money, he needed receipts for everything, even for food from a drive-thru. Leaving for week-ends out of town, or so I was told, only to see him driving with a girl in town as I walked with Shawna to the store to get milk. He would come home finding me crying and ask what my problem was, he would throw things around and again leave out the door laughing. It always being my fault he would say to me and you wonder why I leave, I knew he would use me as an excuse to leave, when really he was leaving all the time anyway. Eventually I would not react to him or a situation, he was going to do as he so pleased so I sat quiet and didn't respond. That too angered him, then he thought I was up to something or was hiding something. It all became crazy, he remained an angry man no matter what, controlling and very cold towards me, and extremely jealous.

I had so many times left him, he would always find me, dragging me back, beating me and taking my clothes off so that I wouldn't run outside to try and get away. One time that didn't even stop me, it was a good thing for me that one time I ran out that way it was 3 o'clock in the morning, all over a bologna sandwich. He sent a man after me once and the message was if I knew what was good for me I'd call home before midnight as a revolver was laying across the seat of the car that the guy was driving. I got the message alright and did call as well as took a bus home the next day, to find some girl with him, he laughing and saying you can go now if you want I've got someone to take care of Shawna. He kept her around for a few days just to let me know he meant business, he told me you can run all you want, I'll always find you. And if it comes down to it I'll have you end up on the streets without a dime, he knew all the right people and all the right lies to tell to make sure of it. Getting in my face nose to nose and say when I get finished with you no one will want you.

The twelve years I stayed with him can hardly be captured on a piece of paper, yet I needed to highlight for you so you could get the picture. All those years, all the threats, all the abuse, all the fear, all the hurt, all that he held against me, I broke from! One day I didn't care anymore if he were to kill me, sometimes I wished he would have, so that I could get away from all the pain and madness.

This day he put forth the straw that broke this camels back, he went for Shawna, we were arguing, she was crying, I was trying to leave the room with her. He grabbed her arm and shoved her into her bedroom. All alone in there she was screaming and crying to come out of her room, he blocking me from going in to get her. I tried to get to her again and again, but he was much larger than I, he always overpowered me. He knew his size intimidated me, I didn't care this time, I grabbed for his face, slugging into the air, I wanted to her. He laughed at me as I tried to get pass him, losing each time, his strength kept me at bay. I could hear her in the room continuing to cry, I yelling for him to open the door so that I could get to her and calm her down. He threw me down and said I had went too far this time, I screamed back at him, that yes he had. The fight was on! Something went off within me when I seen him go for her, which I never thought he would do. I was proven wrong by him that day, yet I knew he was never going to put a hand to her again.

I as usual lost the fight, I laid on the floor when he was finished with me, limp as a rag doll. The sobbing had become a part of my life, trying to catch my breath as I laid there was even so very painful for me. My ribs hurt, my head, my legs, my long hair from being pulled was aching to be released as was I. I felt so alone in it all, as I laid there saying, "Oh God just let me die", I want out.

He walked off towards the family room, I heard the garage door close behind him. I thought as I listened he is getting a gun, he is going to kill me. Remembering the time he took me out in the desert had a gun to my head and said he had to kill me, I knew too much. As I continued to lay there, he wasn't coming back in, all of a sudden I heard a shotgun blast go off. I struggled to get to my feet to go see what had happened. I opened the door and he stood there laughing at me, saying, did you think I had killed myself Kitty? Oh God I cried I want out! I was sickened by it all, I could no longer play such games, especially now that I knew he would go for the girls. Which at that point I knew I could kill over, yet I was always scared he would get up and come after me, or I would end up in prison for attempted murder. That's what he wanted, so I knew I had to get out!

I walked to get Shawna from her room, she too scared to come out or she'd get into trouble. I took her hand and said come on baby lets go take a bath, she was sobbing hard, and Trinity had slept through it all. In he walks and puts a piece of paper on the bathroom counter saying to me this is where I'll be if you need me. But don't call unless it's an emergency, I'm going out of town on some business.

I hear him leave, I listen for the car to back out of the driveway. I get up out of the tub to look at the paper with the number on it, seeing where it was from. The number was from the L.A. area, he was going to be far enough away for me to pack some things and get out, I also knew his business was a woman. I'd pack and give him time to get there, call making sure he was there and not still in town. I had figured he needed an excuse to leave, I didn't care if a woman did answer, it no longer pierced me as it did so many years before. Knowing I had better call to make sure he was really there, and not around the corner watching me. As he had told me many times before, if you ever decide to leave me Kitty and you're not sure where I'm at, you had better watch the headlights in your rearview mirror, they just might be mine. So I called! A woman answered! I asked for my husband, recognizing her voice. Ah! She stammers, not knowing what to say to me. She continues to stutter, stalling for time saying just a minute let me see if he's hear Kitty. I say to her, look don't act stupid, just give him the phone, I hear him in the background asking who was on the phone. She tells him it is me, she asks him if he wants to talk to me, he answers back no! Then I hear him say to her to ask me if its an emergency? I answer to her tell him if me leaving is an emergency enough? And I hang up!

As I walk out the front door with the girls and a few things the phone is ringing off the hook, I just wished I had an answering machine to hear his reply. I close the door behind me, a few clothes no money, yet free from him!

As I drove away the peace in me was overshadowing everything else, I took a big breath and headed for the freeway, I remembered thinking this feels good. Over the years he had always dismissed my feelings for having any value, for I as a person had no value to him, I had become a possession. It was clear to me it was time to get out, away from having this kind a life as an example to my two beautiful girls.

I also knew after I called him I had better get out of town, and be ready to leave, before he had time to call someone to come stop me. Months before I had made a second set of car keys, had hid a gas card, and some change from laundry.

It wasn't much but it was more to me than what I was leaving! As I drove to leave town I stopped at McDonalds to get the girls something to eat! I made my order, got up to the drive-thru window, the manager was at the window, and said to me. The car before you made a wrong order and didn't want it, could you use it instead of us making your order. I was shocked, said yes, thank you! It was doubled of what I ordered, plus it had a Big Mac in there for me! I didn't have enough to order me anything, just the girls. I figured if they were full they would fall asleep for me. It had a large fry, a large soda, a apple pie, I knew it was from God! Only He knew my situation, and He was letting me know He was there all along and would protect me, and see to my needs. We ate as we drove along in the dark night, the sky clear, we could see each star out. We sang songs, they were asleep in no time.

I wanted as far away as I could get, yet as I drove thought where would be the safest place for the girls and I? Right under the nose of his father! He would not try anything too drastic if I lived close to his parents. So I drove into town by his family.

I signed up for emergency assistance till I could get a job, rented a small house. I let his parents know what I had done, asked his dad to call his son and tell him I didn't want any trouble, I just wanted to be left alone. The call must have been made, it was awhile before I heard from him, it was quiet and I felt at ease. Even though we had nothing and were without furniture, it was great!

His dad came over with groceries, and some money. Told me he had told his son to start paying me for the girls, that he didn't like the idea that I was on welfare. I told him thank you, he also said for me to go get some things from the house. To get the girls beds, a T.V., some pots and pans, dishes, linens and toys. Great I told him, I'll find someone to help me with a truck this week-end. He assured me his son would not bother me, it made me feel a little better.

My girl-friend that lived there was able to use her husbands truck that Saturday, so we drove over to get as much as we could in one load. We arrived, the girls visited with their dad as my girl-friend and I loaded. The entire time I watched him with the girls, and he also watched me with eyes of desperation. I could see he was sitting back diagnosing me as well as the situation. As soon as the truck was loaded we were off.

As we drove up to my little house to un-load, his dad was there, making sure we had made it back alright with no trouble.

The next day I had a phone hooked up, I felt un-easy to not be able to call for help if he came around. Yet that night he called! I hadn't even given my phone number out yet! As the phone rang I got sick in my stomach, I thought it's him just letting me know he has my number! I pick it up! It's him! Kitty, he says to me, you just signed your death certificate in a low deep sick voice. I said to him, you don't scare me anymore, and I hung up!

I told his dad the next day, and my husband hated me doing that. My father-in-law assured me it would not happen again. He also told me that he had talked to his son, and realized that he has a bad temper and told me that it scared me when he went for Shawna. He too knew it was better for us to be apart until this all blew over. He suggested that I finish getting my things from the house and bring them here with me. I told him I would as soon as I could find another week-end free and someone to help me. I was working now at home watching the children of some school teachers. My father-in-law said my son has friends over there where he lives to help you, I'll call him and see.

There was a guy that my husband found to help me. So I got to town, loaded up his truck, had Trinity in the cab with me. My husband drove in front of us with Shawna. Onto the freeway we went, I looked out into the pitch black night and sighed a breath of relief for it felt good to be out, or so I thought!

A ways down the freeway sparks were coming out of the underneath part of the dashboard. As we continued to drive I started to smell smoke. I asked this guy do you see that, what is it? Do you smell smoke? No! He said no! Trinity asleep in my arms in the cab of the truck, I became frightened and told him to pull over. We had lost our Motorhome to fire last year and it had burned to the ground within minutes. As he pulled over my hand was on the door handle, Trinity in my arms, I jumped out of the truck and ran into the dark night off to the side to what I thought was a clearing.

Next thing I know I was falling with my baby in my arms!

"UNABLE TO MOVE"

I was at the bottom of a ditch, I could only see the dark sky above as I heard nothing as I layed there. I was unable to move, in such pain but I tried to call to Trinity. I couldn't hear her little voice at all. I could hardly breathe, the pressure on my back and chest was enormous. My stomach felt hot, and my head was so painful I just wanted to cry. Yet I couldn't I had to call out to her once more, with little puffs of breath I pushed out her name. Trinity! I listened! Trinity! I whispered, my voice faint. Again, Trinity! Nothing! I now find myself starting to cry. It so painful to even do that. One more time I cried, Trinity come to mama, over here baby! Still nothing but silence all around me.

Deep within I pray! For I had no more verbal words to utter. Oh God! You see Trinity at this moment, help her Lord! If she is injured in any way give it all to me, please don't let her be in pain. I know you can do this, Lord.

I layed there still with the silence of the night covering me. Listening! Still nothing! With gasps of air I call her and cry out! God! A dark mist is gathering at my feet, I lay there helpless and motionless. I continued to talk to the Lord. It was getting hard for me to breathe at all now, with the pressure across my chest and stomach now tremendous.

I cry deep within, don't let her die Lord! I know you see us and can bring us through. Trinity I softly cry, Trinity, come here baby! The darkness now not only at my feet but it now is moving towards me, a heaviness comes to my chest. It feels as though my breath is being taken from me. Again deep within I cry! Jesus! Jesus! Jesus!

God come help us! At that moment the darkness surrounding me lifted, it all became light around me, like a flash had went off. It lit up the sky! The heaviness also lifted off me, I take a big breath and push out "Trinity", one more time.

I felt a slight little touch come across my cheek, a tiny hand to my face touching me. I hear, don't cry mommy! Don't cry mommy as she wiped away my tears that were falling to the ground. The tears were hot as they streamed down my face, into my ears and neck, my eyes swollen now. She layed next to me, putting her little arms around my shoulder and she too now started crying. I whisper to her, it's O.K. baby, Jesus is here with us now.

Someone yells from atop the ditch, I hear a baby crying down here, come flash your lights down here. The lights shined down on us, and the ropes began to be thrown down to us. Men began to hover around us, they remove Trinity from my side. I continue to pray, for the Lord to hold on to me and be my strength.

A man comes to me and asks my name, I can't answer, the pain now more than I can bear. Lets get her out of here he yells to the others. They begin to get down to me, and determine my injuries. They think I'm pregnant because my stomach is distended from the fall, I have internal injuries and am bleeding. They get me in the basket to lift me out, I can feel myself slumping forward, I have no muscle or strength to hold myself up or in. It was a frightening thing to feel nothing as they pulled me up to the level ground above me.

I thought of Trinity as they sat me down, as they were lifting me into the ambulance. A paramedic saw that I was trying to say something and bent over closer to hear. I whisper, where is my baby? Has anyone seen her baby, he yells to the others! Another paramedic yells back, she's fine her dad has her.

I was now not only physically numb I was emotionally numb as well. I cried as I was lifted into the ambulance, I knew she was not fine in his arms. I arrive at the Hospital, I'm run through tests, machines, xrays, blood taken. A brace is put on my neck, back and leg, I had torn ligaments, crushed vertabraes. I had stretched parts of my body I didn't even know of, or could I say their names. My body still swollen from the fall and internal injuries remained, I was put on oxygen to help me breathe, and a catheter in me, and I was hooked up to everything but freedom.

As I layed there in my bed in the Hospital, I heard a man talking to the nurse at my door. She states to him, poor thing she'll probably never walk again! Oh! He replies to her, you don't know Kitty! As he came in I could tell from his voice it was the Parish Priest, don't you look pretty he says to me with a wink!

Don't make me laugh I tell him it even hurts to laugh! You better laugh he says, it's the only thing you got going for you. Plus the word says, "a merry heart does good like a medicine". He then says to me, Kitty you have two choices either stay like this or beat the odds against you and get up! Do you understand what I'm saying to you, he asks? Yes, I answered, I know exactly what your saying to me. Good he says lets pray that God will extend His healing hand over, in and through your body. He left that day after we prayed, I could feel the strength well up within me, I was encouraged!

As the days followed, I was hooked up, strapped down, linked to, braced in and I wasn't going anywhere too soon. Yet within me I knew the time and day would come. The days past, with nurses coming in to bathe me, brush my teeth and hair. Each day to turn my limp body from side to side, putting lotion on me, and taking new tests. The food was yummy I thought to myself, only if I could taste it as it dripped down a tube and into my arms.

I remained flat on my back, daring not to even sneeze for that too caused me some pain. The ceiling and I became good friends, it listened each night as I talked to God.

My husband came in one day to inform me that he had all my things moved back to his house, he didn't think I'd be going back there any time soon. The days turned into weeks, I could see my girls through an outside window, when and if my husband brought them. I would smile to them out from my bed, Shawna trying to be so grown up, and Trinity waving big with a picture she had made for me. The Doctors didn't believe she fell with me that night, there was not a scratch on her body, not even a sticker in her hair. At night I thanked God for what He did for her and I that evening. For I know way deep inside death wanted us both. I could not only sense it, I smelled it moving about, you can feel it's presence.

My healing process would now continue at home, the Hospital was releasing me to my husbands care. Still unable to move, turn, get up, potty on my own, hold a hair brush, or really keep food down because of my internal injuries, I was helpless. Yet I went, this too God used to heal me, it made me stronger and build faith, endurance and strength within me.

A few days went by, the ambulance is taking me back to where I had ran from, and now I had to face it all over again. Only this time I had not one single part of my body to help me, for it was not budging. I remained to have braces on me, my vertabraes in my lower back were unhealed, the torn ligaments in my left knee and my right foot weren't healed either. Therapy would continue, I knew that if I couldn't make it here, I'd never make it.

As the ambulance pulls up to the house, the rear door opens, they pull me out on the bed, which has collapsed wheels and legs unfold to roll me in with. As I roll down the sidewalk my two beautiful girls are out on the grass anxiously waiting to get to me, and I to them. The house looks the same, dark, depressing and cold, it was all him. The same dark leather sofa, an old recliner sat in front of the T.V., with his remote on the arm of his chair. And there in the middle of it all sat my hospital bed waiting for me, as if it was made to be there too.

They transferred me over to my bed, my husband signed for the bill, and they were gone. That night was horrible for me, he sent the girls to bed after dinner, turned the lights out where I was, and went to his room. The morning came with no difference, everyone remained to tip-toe around to not disturb him. It was for me death, I was laying in the middle of all that I came to want to get away from, now it all surrounded me. It little by little ate at me. I layed there and tears so hot from the pain inside would fall down my face. It all incased me in a tomb of unbelief, I remembered the scripture, that God never gives us more than we can handle. I would ponder over that saying and ask, Oh Lord do you really know me? Do you see me so different than I see myself, you believe I can handle all this?

The third night home, I cried myself to sleep, it was all so hopeless. I felt as though my heart were to burst if not to totally die, all I dreamed of gone from me. It was all held now in one bad dream after another. I couldn't get away from it all, it was ever so apparent and real to me as I layed there unable to even go to the bathroom on my own. If I sneezed my nose remained to run, if I cried the tears remained to fall and stain my face. The room so dark, shadows hid in every corner, the wind blew through the fireplace screen like someone else was crying too. A ever so slight whimper coming to my ears, at first I thought it was my echo. The silence of the night was engulfing me in fears I couldn't protect myself from, I remained to lay helpless and alone.

I was waken by a tiny little hand rubbing the side of my cheek, it was Trinity. "Don't cry mommy" she said, can I sleep with you? Yes baby I tell her, put your feet up on this bar and pull yourself up, put your leg over it now and tuck yourself in. She does it all and snuggles in to fit my form as I layed there motionless unable to help her or to hold her. The warmth of her love made me sleep as if I didn't have a care. At that moment she was what I needed. God is so good I remembered saying as I fell off to sleep with my baby next to me.

We were woken up the next morning to my husband telling Trinity to get out of the bed with me. I tell him she's fine let her lay here with me! He leans into my face and says, let's get one thing straight, nothing has changed around here.

My heart sunk! In a low voice I answer. That's right it hasn't and soon as I get out of this bed, I am out of here with my girls. He laughed! Saying you really think your gonna walk again? Yes I tell him! Your not going anywhere he replies, and walks off. Trinity runs over and kisses my hand through the bed rails and runs to play.

The day was cold as was the feeling coming from him to me. That night as I again layed there in the dark room I again talked to God. Lord I know I'm not suppose to go by what I see or how I feel. But I can see what I look like, and I feel nothing! Help me please Lord! Show me the way out!

Deep within me a voice said, "take the blanket in your right hand and squeeze"! I say back in my head, how am I going to do that Lord? I can't see my hand to move it, or even know if it is there. "You don't have to". Oh Lord I said, I am sorry! I forgot it's by faith not by what I see or feel!

Alright I thought to myself I will do this. I will take the blanket in my right hand and begin to by faith squeeze it in the palm of my hand. I night after night after night do this by faith, I tell no one. Over and over I repeat it each evening as everyone is in bed.

About two weeks past, this one night I was told, "now take your right hand and crawl it up the side rail to it's top". Still only remaining to look up at the ceiling I in faith move my hand to this position. I still didn't see it or feel it moving any where. I kept it up night after night. Oh God I cried! I can't do this it's not working for me! I fell into a thought of hopelessness!

By faith see it, I thought. Alright I'll close my eyes and see it in there. I now put my trust in Him and rise up in faith. Putting my hand in His and by faith I'll see my hand going up the side rail. As I closed my eyes I could see it, I could see my hand over to the side going up in my mind, it was moving!

I was so excited I started to giggle and my eyes came opened. Over to the side, I saw my hand on the siderail! I was laughing so hard I began to cry. Oh God! It was working all along, the whole time just like you said!

I didn't have to see it in order for it to work huh? How silly of me! I am sorry Lord!

From that point on there was no stopping me, by faith I continued to now move to my left hand, moving from side to side. I now knew it wasn't me doing it anyway, it was the gift of faith that was being built up in me!

One night I take my right hand as well as my left hand, and move them at the same time. Inch by inch I move them forward on the side-rail of the hospital bed, I can feel myself coming up to a sitting position. I feel the extreme pressure on my lower back, so I slowly go down. I repeat this too, over and over each night for the next few days. I can feel myself getting stronger, my hands can easily now move up the rails.

So now this night I keep going with both hands on the side-rails, little by little, inch by inch I move my hands slowly forward. Again I am coming up to a sitting position. You can do it I tell myself, come on! I'm up! Now what I think to myself? What are you gonna do now? I can't hold myself up, I start to fall forward! This is fun I think, it's three o'clock in the morning and here I am in a hospital bed in the middle of my living room laughing!

My laughing topples me over face first into the covers, I'm motionless! I still remain to giggle even though I'm stuck. The hall light comes on! Oh Oh! I think to myself, I think I woke him! What are you doing he says? Ah! I had to use the restroom! It was not at all funny to him, since he and I knew I remained to use a bed-pan. He put me back down on my back, and went back to bed. I just thought the entire thing was funny! I laughed all night! That was the night I took to heart and realized the "Joy" of the Lord was truly going to be my strength.

Each night I went further and further, I started to wiggle my feet and toes, extending all my toes out in order for my calf muscle to be strengthened. It took time to get to each part of my body, but time is one thing I did have. One step at a time, and I was going! I knew if I didn't start to move soon, atrophy would set in.

One day a friend came over to see me, and as usual to help, encourage and pray, I showed her what I had been doing, she was dancing around saying "Glory". She was more excited than I, she helped me sit up and move my legs off to the side of the bed. I had never seen my legs like that before, they were pitiful, all skinny and gray looking. I was horrified to see the condition of my body. I started to cry as she sat me up.

All of a sudden she yelled "Devil you can't have her you're a liar"! Man oh man, if she didn't scare him she sure made me shake! Come on she said your getting up! I was excited to see her and all, but I felt like I was in boot camp and she was my drill sergeant! I was laughing again! Come on she said lets get down into this wheel-chair and I'll take you on a grand tour.

Well I was sitting to the side of the bed alright, like a limp rag doll still. She then says I'll help you, I'll put my arms around your rib cage and lift you down into the wheel-chair. Oh boy I thought, even though it wasn't very far down it was a scary thought to me. I didn't ever want to fall again. She could see the fear on my face. "Devil" she yelled again!

Alright, alright I said let's go! Well I was down and in, she tucked some pillows in around to hold me up. Let's go for a spin she said! Let's go I said! We were off, a grand tour of the house, from kitchen to bedrooms, it all looked the same. I knew then I wouldn't be staying in that wheel-chair for long either. She became a much needed prayer warrior in my life at that time, again God knew exactly what I needed.

I went through each step as God granted me strength daily. I went from the wheel-chair, to a walker, to crutches, to a cane to crawling. The crawling for me was the easiest, it made me stronger faster. I had to use my body to move when I crawled around. The other things hampered me, and only kept me depended on them for my mobility. At times I just layed helpless on the floor and cried.

Months now past, it is Christmas. The Parish Priest calls and asks me, you coming to church? Yes I say! My husband loads me in the car, wheel-chair and all. We are off, Trinity is excited I am finally going out. We get there, he unloads me and sits me in the wheel-chair, we go inside. I have not been in there since I was hurt. It seems like all eyes are on me, I have him put me towards the front so I wouldn't block the isle.

It comes time for communion, the Priest looks over to me and motions his head for me to get up and come partake. My eyes become huge and I get a huge smile across my face. In me I know I can do it. His eyes again to me smiling with a come on message in them. O.K. God! Lets go, its you and me! You be my strength and I'm up and to the front.

I put the lock on the wheel-chair and up my body went, unsteady yet up! I was standing, no crutches, no walker, no cane, I began! My feet shuffled across the floor, I could not lift them, I had no strength but to move forward. I depended totally upon Him to be my strength, for I had none on my own, I leaned on my Father in faith to take me forward.

I kept my eyes focused on the Priest, as he looked at me coming towards him, with a bigger grin than mine. I had made it! As I stood there with my hands outstretched to receive communion, he says to me, "Body of Christ Kitty, eat and be made whole"! I did, I was and I am!

From that day forward I was never the same woman, I had gained a sense of strength from within that I had never encountered till that moment. My endurance out weighed my strength, I came to the realization that it was His life I was partaking of and not my own.

As the days continued I was able to move from my wheel-chair to slowly working myself around the house, using the walls to balance me. I would use furniture as resting places as I moved around trying to clean, I crawled to the cabinets under the kitchen sink to get the rag and cleanser to clean the bathtub. If the phone rang I would pull it down off the counter to answer it, when I was alone I'd keep it down on the floor. I tired easily, still so frail in many ways. Being exhausted became a daily routine for me, yet I kept going. I was not about to give up, I had a hope risen in me to take me anywhere I wanted. I knew my healing was a gift from God, this too was to be for His glory! I found out that by the grace of God go I!

I had learned to stand at the sink and do dishes, brush my girls hair and my own, I even graduated to being potty trained, at the time my biggest wish come true. I had lost weight and muscle mass, my legs were so weak, and my hands were unsteady as they regained remembrance of simple household chores.

I sat on the edge of the tub to bathe, afraid to get in, for the fear of falling. My bodily strength unable to hold me long, so I learned quickly to improvise, I was not going to be an invalid unable to live an active normal life. At the end of the day I was seriously in need of a bed, rest was beyond the need at that time.

Once in bed, I would reflect back at how I took each movement of my body for granted, the simple tasks of just getting up to shower now took me up to an hour to complete. To hold something in my hand, to stand, let alone to walk, to lay in a comfortable position and not be in pain. To have someone wash my body, brush my teeth, shave my legs, empty my bed-pan! All now a common occurrence in my life, of which I never wanted to go back to, so this kept my mobility forefront in my life on a daily basis, moment by moment.

The struggle now was to rest in Him healing me, and providing this new life for me as well as a new walk. I had so depended upon myself before, this trial took me to a place of realizing I had nothing of my own to depend upon.

Yet as I became stronger, not only physically but spiritually, it seemed as if my husband weakened. He often looked scared, he was less than happy with my progress.

I was very grateful for the renewed life in me, daily I was thankful and would never again take for granted the mobility I now was given. Again a gift!

My husbands slight remarks continued, belittled, made to feel less than, only remarks to hinder me and not encourage. I couldn't look at it, I had to move forward. I was just along for the ride, as he so often told me. He would make me aware of the many women that now accommodated his wishes. Within me that was taken from me years ago, it mattered not to me of his escapades with other women now. I was still in a condition of wonder of what was happening around me spiritually, I gave him no mind when he intentionally now tried to hurt me. This was for him madness, as I stood silent as he told me where he had been and who he had been with.

I continued to pray for us, a healing between the two of us was desperately needed. I felt alone. His fits of rage were common place in our life now, he only seemed to worsen. There was a day I would try to figure out why he would get so angry, no more! I had finally come to the conclusion, no reason, he just did! I had always heard it took two to tango! Let me tell you it does not, he was dancing all on his own.

The day came when he kept pushing me into a corner, literally with his finger in my chest, pointing over and over against me. He was trying to pin me up against the wall, the veins in his neck bulging, his eyes huge and red, fists clenched, face bursting with anger. I knew those were all signs to retreat! To get out of his way, for I feared if he ever put a hand to me now, I'd be disabled for sure. I tried to maneuver myself out of his reach.

He had over the years enjoyed pinning me up against the wall, but at this time I had no where to go. My body was still hampered in so many ways. He liked to watch me look frightened like a caged animal, sensing the attack tries to find a way out. Yet, escape eludes them! This was I at that very moment!

He kept at me, pushing me backwards into the wall. Stabbing me in the chest continuously with his finger, over and over. I could feel I was about to lose my balance.

I again deep in my spirit call upon the Lord. Come help me! Protect me! Put your protective angels about me once again! I stood in silence as he continued to prod me.

A voice came deep from within, "It's a bluff"! He is scared of you! "What?" I thought. It looks like he is getting ready to kill me. I can feel something within me begin to well up, I didn't feel frightened of him anymore. I thought he is never going to do this to me again. I stood there, he was still in my face. He with a glare of death on his face, so familiar that look had become.

It welled up in me and all of sudden just came out, I say to him! You don't scare me anymore! You have tried to kill me all this time and were never able to. Try it now, I told him, go ahead! You have hurt no one but yourself all these years, you have become your own worst enemy! No one has done a thing to you, you are on your way to no where! And where has it all gotten you?

His eyes remaining to glare into mine. I still am in his face, he will not move. I then say to him, you have bragged all these years, you've never met your match! There is no one as big and strong as you! That you are afraid of nothing and no one!

I tell him now. You had better be afraid, you better be afraid of one person and that is "God". His eyes losing there glare. I tell him, there is a God and nothing I could ever do to you, could compare with what you have to answer for. I hope you believe that. Then I say or maybe the devil scares you? Cause that is who you have been listening to. And who is behind all the garbage these years.

He is now standing shoulders down and remaining to look at me. I tell him, what has it all been for? Where has it gotten you? What was the problem? You have two beautiful daughters, a nice home, a good job, terrific friends, your family, and me. I have stood by you all these years, for better or worse. What was it? Just what is the problem?

He is still! He now begins to back up to the chair behind him and sits down. Staring at the floor he says to me, I've lost you haven't I Kitty? The look on his face makes me want to give in, he looks like a little scared boy!

I started to cry. "What did you expect? You can't treat me like this and believe it is all fine." I tell him "it reminds of the way you used to treat our hound dogs, do you remember I ask?" "Yes" he says. I call it, kick the dog theory! He asks me why? I tell him you would get mad for no reason and call the dogs to you, they would come with fear in there eyes, bellies to the ground and wetting all over themselves. They didn't trust you! Then when they got to you, you'd put a chain around there necks and swing them above your head, letting them go into the tree. Do you remember? "Yes" he said!

I would watch you from the up-stairs window. I'd run down crying and beg for you to stop! You'd look at me and laugh, say "they deserve it, they are stupid." Stupid for coming back to me for more, and trusting me! "That's me huh?" I ask him with my eyes full of tears, the pain so real as I re-captured it in my memory.

I have remembered it all, all you said all you did. All those years I felt like those dogs, like them I thought you'd change too. Like them I loved you too! And all for what? Such a senseless game you have played with us!

Like the time you beat me and as I layed on the bed, you'd come in to say "I'm sorry" apologizing to me! Every time I believed you, you'd be nice. I would again give in to the moment of kindness you would show me. Only for you to take advantage of me by putting a pillow over my head trying to suffocate me. Laughing and saying "you're stupid Kitty, you're too trusting." You deserve to die.

He continues to look at the ground. I tell him all it did was make me want to distance myself from you. "I never knew what to expect from you. I still don't, and all for what?" "It has only served to tear us apart!" I could tell by the look on his face he knew he had lost his hold over me. I too knew he would never again hold me with fear of what he would do to me. His threats to me were now worthless.

I go to bed, in with the girls as usual. For it had been sometime since we had slept as husband and wife. I had nothing left in me to give. I had become numb to it all, it was gone from me years ago. Never to be recaptured for us, it was all truly sad to watch over the years.

The next day as he was at work, I left again. I packed the girls things, I knew it would get ugly, but I had to get out. For his survival as well as mine and the girls. We were only dying a slow death staying like that, it did no one any good.

I didn't tell him this time where I was, I even had to keep Shawna out of school for I knew he would pick her up and use her as leverage to get to me. We would stay hid this time, at a friends in a back room. He had threats all over town to people he knew I still had contact with. He threatened me with divorce, to take the girls from me, and the house, leaving me on the street. He would leave messages with friends telling them what to tell me, and what he was going to do to me. Telling others of how he would leave me on the streets to die. To break my bones and my body would be broken beyond repair. My faced sliced, my teeth bashed out, he would drag me behind his truck in the desert, leaving me to die.

People were so afraid of what he was telling them, I was the one encouraging them. I had some refuse to help me because they were so afraid of him. I was not going back, even if I had to run out of state and hide I would have, not because of fear but because of my girls. Not for fear that he would kill me, for deep within I had died a thousand deaths through the years.

Notes were left on the car I drove, letting me know that he knew where I was. Telling me to watch who I talked to, because people always had a price, even my friends and family. So I stayed to myself, I knew he was being fed information from both sides.

Once at the grocery store the girls and I came out, and he had come and taken the car. Bags in hand we walked, in plain view of everyone, right down main street we went. People would stop to see if we needed a ride. He was watching it all from a short distance behind, later he'd call and say was that your boyfriend that gave you a ride? You are sick I told him, remember he said, I've been at this longer than you have. I know how to get people, and I know what to say, even if I have to lie, you will lose! I hung up! The phone continued to ring, it made him crazy not to have my full attention. He would drive by, pull over and say, you'll pay for this Kitty. I told him, "send me the bill, you know where I live". He was livid, he now knew he was truly the loser.

He had men he worked with try and pick me up, try to come on to me, just to see what I'd do. Even on the phone, telling me you really need to go back to him. I just kept hanging up!

He called and said, you can run, you can hide, but you will never get away from me. No matter where you go, what you do, you will lose in the end. He said that I might as well come back to him, or I'd find myself buried six feet under. I told him, you don't get it do you? I am not coming back, I am not afraid of you, I am never going to live like that again! I again hung up!

He became ill after I left, heart problems and anger was getting the best of him. He was eventually not able to drive, or get around. He was not listening to anyone, not even his doctors. He was not about to give in.

I would take the girls over to see him, I'd do some laundry for him, we'd have sandwiches with him. He was growing weaker and weaker daily. Once I came over to help him around the house, and he was still in his pajamas, too weak to get dressed. The holidays were coming up, he wanted the girls for Christmas, I told him I'd think about it. We checked on him occasionally through out the weeks that followed. He was seeing his doctors in L.A. on Thursdays, but he still wouldn't listen.

He called me, tells me he is going to his mom's for Christmas, she was driving up to get him. He still wanted the girls, and asked if they can come with them. I say yes, of course! He is silent on the other end! He tells me thanks!

School is out, I get the girls things together, explain they will go with their daddy to grama's for Christmas. Shawna is not too pleased, and Trinity is not happy at all. I tell them to go, they will have fun, daddy is sick and needs them. They cry and say no! They eventually give in, but want me to come too! I tell them no, this is just special time for them and daddy. If I came I would only get in the way. Plus I told them, grama and daddy had bought them really special presents. For them to go and have fun, and we would have our Christmas when they returned, and that I would call them everyday and night. They were fine with that, and helped me put their things in the car.

We drove up to his house and his mom was already there waiting. I helped to get the girls and their things into her car, they were staring me in the eye, looking as though I might change my mind. I hugged them, told them bye and I'd call them tonight. They were off!

It was all I could do to let them go, to walk away and not keep them all to myself. No matter what he had done, I could not in return be like that to him, inside we both really knew I did love him. That is why I had to do this, I had to trust God no matter what. And I did have a peace about letting them go.

I got into my car to leave, and it was all I could do to make it around the corner. I had to pull over. I slumped over the steering wheel and wept for sometime, it was awful to be without my girls. I waited to call that night, everything seemed to be going well. Except Trinity is crying for me, and it angers her dad and grama that she wants me, and Shawna tells me she is trying to keep her out of their way. I ask him what happened why is Trinity crying? He says to me, she's wanting you, and cries all the time. I tell him, she is a baby, she's only three years old, don't be hard on her. I get the girls back on the phone, she calms down for me, and Shawna says she will watch her. We say good night and I hang-up again crying myself to sleep.

The days go by slowly, I go to friends for dinner, I try and stay brave, but inside I am falling apart. I feel as though he and his family are up to something, yet again I have to erase it from my mind. I go to bed after calling the girls, it is now after Christmas Eve, they are excited to come home.

I go to bed, feeling lonely, and empty. I assure myself to go to sleep and in the morning all will be well, then the next day they will come home.

I do get to sleep, yet restless all night, wake up with cold sweats, I feel frightened for some reason. I lay back down, still un-easy. It's late but I want to call my girls, something is wrong! It's too late, wait till morning. I again lay back down, having a horrible dream. I'm awakened by someone at the door.

Reaching to open the door, it is a friend of my husbands from work. I feel sick, cold and now know something is wrong.

Kitty, he says, your husband died last night, at his mom's house!

"The Last Slap"

Numb with the news, in more than a state of shock, even unable to cry, it is beyond belief for me. The man remains to talk as I stare out into space, I close the door as he walks away. I begin to cry, not for myself, but for my husband. Oh God, I cry! Now what?

My car is broken, I have no money, I need to go get my girls, I'm a total mess, and now have to go out of town to face this situation.

I get a ride, it is night before we arrive at his family's house out of town. I go in but I can sense I'm not welcomed, all the years of what he had done to me erased from their minds. All they knew was that he was dead and they blamed that on me too! They were not letting go the time I left him, their faces with words unspoken, yet riddled with questions unanswered.

No turning back now I thought to myself as I sat my things down in the back bedroom, we had to move forward, or at least I knew I had to, especially for my girls. I could not afford to stay in such a place that would soon kill me too! It was clear in what I had to do, mentally, emotionally, spiritually, and physically. I could feel as it tried to grip my very soul, tearing at me from within to consume my very presence. I could not let it have me, I saw what hate, bitterness, pride, and not to forgive others had done around me for years. I could not succumb to it, it would slowly take my life from within. As I sat on the edge of the bed I could feel it as it tried to hold me in a place of wanting to lash out, I wanted to blow it all up in my mind. I had to move away from it quickly, such destruction awaited me if I took its path. I could not go to it as it called me to come to its arms of despair, I would not surrender to its call, now or ever.

After the funeral I was given my husbands "Will", in a long white un-addressed envelope. What it contained I would soon find out would be the most excruciating time of my life, its contents for me held a silent scream that no one could hear nor perceive, nor did I care to share with those around. It was contained so deep within me that day and for some time to come, it was deafening to my ears, my heart, my soul.

I gathered my girls belongings, and we headed home, some how I treasured the long drive home this time. The drive was never ending to me, my girls fell asleep, and the quietness led me to retrace the piece of paper I was given. The Will! Stating he leaves his mom as executor of the estate, to sell everything and pay his bills, he acknowledges that Shawna and Trinity are his daughters, and states to my wife Kitty, I leave the sum of one dollar ($1.00), no more and no less.

That piece of paper read to me was a valueless consideration for life, caring nothing for life, others or themselves. All worthless on his part, the struggle on his part to maintain power was a driving force even in his death, it was all so very sad!

My life, the years I stayed with him, was worth one dollar! It was not the money I cared about it was the intent behind the statement, and my husband knew that. He knew this would be his last slap to me, even in his death. Reaching from the grave to get to me, to kill me, to bury me in it all. I shook as I thought of the useless ugly intent of the evil that was behind it.

The road ahead went on forever, the blackness of the night seemed to engulf me. The night was as I, dark and silent and passed by without a thought, yet there! I held back the tears, I wanted my girls to not know a thing of this, my body acting as if it were without emotion. I couldn't seem to catch my breath, how silly of my husband to continue to try and kill me, didn't he know I was already dead. He had stripped me of everything I ever dreamed of, gone!

The person I was, who I was trying to hold on to, I didn't know her either. She was just a reaction performing in a shell of a body, just going through the motions hoping to get to the end of another day.

We pull into town, I could see there were lights on in the house as we drive up. I walk up with the girls and there suitcases in hand, I reach for the house keys and put it into the lock on the front door. It turns and the door opens only to be held partly by a chain lock coming across the housekeepers face as she peers out. She tells me, I can't let you in Kitty! I walk across the street and ask the couple if I could please use there phone, of course they reply, are you alright, the lady asks?

I call a mutual friend of my husbands and mine also, at that time I knew I could count on him for help. He can tell I'm hurting and tells me he is on the next plane out of New York bound for California, he assured me he'd be here by morning.

I ask the couple across the street if my girls and I could spent the night with them till morning, they are very hospitable and agree, they are especially excited to have my girls over. The woman begins laying out fresh towels on the counter, running water in the bathtub. Then she tells my girls to enjoy their bath, she would turn their beds down and fix a little snack for them after they were finished. How sweet I thought to myself as I watched them prepare everything so nicely for us, we were guests and she treated us as family. Later on I realized her lifestyle was to treat family as guests and to treat guests as family. I never forgot that, and would soon find out their age and experience in life held so much for me as well as for my girls to learn from as time passed.

We wake to the smell of freshly brewed coffee filling the warmth of their home. She tenderly comes into the room where I had slept and asks would you like to take a shower, she has everything laid out for me. She then lets me know I can use her special lotion and when I'm finished to come and have breakfast with them, my girls were already up and helping to set the table.

As I went into the bathroom, it was all so sweet to me, her gentleness overwhelmed me at that moment. I stepped into the hot shower, its steam already gathered on the bathroom mirror as to seem a fog had set in. Which was fine with me for I didn't care to clearly see myself at that time. As I stood under the water, I hoped as it ran over my body that it would rinse off all the debris that had accumulated over the years.

I shut the shower off and now ran the tub, I was weakened by the past few days I had to relax. The soaking was wonderfully welcomed, its warmth captivating my senses as I sunk down and went under water. Taking away all sounds and all that now my mind was holding on to, washing it clear of all that I wanted to let go of.

Her lotion filled the bathroom with its scent without me even opening it as yet, smelling of honey and almonds, mixed with a delicate blend of oils straight from the orient I thought as I opened it.

That smell was quickly overshadowed as bacon and eggs came into my nostrils, a knock at the door letting me know breakfast was on, would I like to have my coffee black or with cream and sugar she asks. I'm coming out now I answer to her, with cream and sugar please.

After breakfast I settled down with a cup of coffee and we all chatted, it was good for me to see my girls enjoying themselves with the couple. It was a great change for me and much needed, it took my mind off all that seemed to pull me away. We finished up the breakfast dishes, made our beds, cleaned up the bathroom and thanked them both, we had a delightful stay, I told them.

I go across the street to wait for my company to arrive, he pulls up within 10 minutes, he goes to the door with me. The house-keeper explains to him as well that I can not come in, he tells her she had better open the door or he will take it off its hinges. She tells him she will call the police. Good he says, maybe they and the newspaper would like the story of why you are keeping her and her children out of their home. We are let in, she is escorted out. He goes and has all new locks put on the doors, gives me the keys to the house and tells me you have any other trouble you have my phone number.

His daughter is getting married out of town he tells me and you need a break, you and the girls want to come along? Trinity pops up with a big, yes! We go and had a fantastic time, the wedding was beautiful, the food all Italian, the music also, mixed with a little pop of the day. My girls danced away the hours on top of his feet, giggled and ran around with the other children, with flowers in their hair from the decorations off the tables. I sit there and visit with friends I hadn't seen in years, the week-end quickly comes to a close, he drives us back home.

He comes in for a minute to visit to see that all is alright, he and his wife are leaving and we all give hugs, you call us they say if you need anything.

We were in our home once again, yes we were in alright and what the next seven years held for me as I went through probate was a less than pleasant experience.

We had no money coming in, the house was in foreclosure and all our utilities were turned off, the couple across the street lent us a ice-chest and a flashlight. The couple bought us some milk, cereal, bologna and bread for sandwiches, and an occasional treat for the girls. They quickly became my girls Grandma and Grandpa, they also let us come over each evening and bathe and he cooked them breakfast each morning before Shawna got off to school. After that Trinity came with me in a wagon and I went around to look for cleaning jobs so to get some money for food. I had no money to pay any bills even to keep the house going, everything was tied up in court. His retirement checks didn't clear for months. But even if I made a few dollars a day I could stop at the store on the way home and pick up some groceries for the girls. We would be finished by the time Shawna was out of school each day, sometimes she would go finish up a job with us, to her and Trinity it was again another adventure. We turned in at night early, especially not having lights made night set in very soon.

After my husbands retirement started coming in it became retroactive from the past months, so I turned everything back on got my house payments paid up. The head manager at my banking establishment where the house was held was a very gracious man while I went through it all. I explained to him my situation and he held all papers on foreclosure for some months, again God knew exactly the man to be there for me at that time. It took some calls before I reached a listening ear to help me, he had the last say so over everyone I had talked to. I took the chain of command till I finally reached him, I even gave him the phone number of the friends I was calling from in case he needed to reach me. He was more than understanding with me and at times would call my friends just to see how I was doing.

It was all extremely hard for me, my body was not totally healed as yet, yet each day I pushed myself to get up. Papers continued to be filed, things sold, court dates to keep, work to go to, Shawna in school and Trinity with me. I had so very much to content with, along with my physical body still being hampered and not totally healed, at times I would find myself grieving for my husband. Especially when I looked upon our two beautiful daughters, realizing all that he would miss throughout their upcoming years. My head swirled at it all, some days I found it hard to know where to begin, other times I couldn't move, my foot would give way toppling me to the ground, where on some days I stayed for the day.

Yet each day He remained faithful with me, taking me through even though physically I was contending with a load I know I could have never carried without Him. He was ever proving He was my provider, my sustainer, my healer, my counselor, my Father and friend.

One evening as I laid on my bed resting I cried out once again to my faithful listener. Oh God! I don't need to tell you what is happening to me, you see it all, as well as know it all. My husband not only abused me in his life but in his death as well. It all seems as a bad dream, I'm trying to keep my head up Lord! My body is worsening, my foot is now beginning to drag off to the side, my back is in constant pain, I don't sleep even at night, my knee is swollen with pain cause I don't stay off my feet, the money is not enough, I can't drive even if I did have a car. Court continues, looking into my girls eyes each day for they fear I would get worse then what would happen to them, they ask?

I trust you Lord, you are all I have you know that, you are the lifter of my head, my strength to go on, my shield of protection about me. Hold me up Lord, don't let me go under, don't let me give up hope! Hear my cry Oh Lord!

It was extremely quiet! He spoke ever so softly within me. "Yes my child all this has happened, now what are you to do with it?"

I knew He was asking for my response to it all! His stillness surrounded me, I knew at that moment I had to make a choice. Either now move in what He wanted of me, or to live in self pity, revenge, hatred, regrets, and a life of bitterness, and not forgive!

As it remained to be ever so still I pondered on it all. He now placed it before me. What was I to do?

Then without speaking He brought to my mind, my favorite man in scripture. Joseph! After all that was done to him, he always made the right response. God had answered me! I sat still on my bed and let Him have it all, for it could be mine if I chose to hang on to it, yet I asked for His answer for mine would be wrong, I knew.

Thank you Lord I said as I sat there, thanks for showing Joseph to me, you knew I liked his story in the Bible the best, and would some day use it to be my example. After all was said and done to Joseph he continued to have the right response, no matter what was done to him even from his own family, he never moved in a bad response towards them. He held his heart in a place always useable by you, in fact years later when his family was brought before him for food, they not knowing who Joseph was, nor the position that his God had raised him to.

Joseph had to go behind the curtain as he wept bitterly for he loved his family, meant them no harm even though they wanted him dead. He only wanted to be restored to them, all along keeping a right attitude and response before his God.

His families feelings of jealousy towards him was used for bad intent yet God turned it for His good.

This I know is what God is looking at from us as well, what is our response to what has happened to us? Do we have a right attitude? The right response? Joseph as Jesus knew it was God's hand upon his life, their will was for God's will to be performed through their life.

As I do so will for my life, for I now know what He holds for me is beyond compare to anything that is brought my way in this journey of a life. I like Joseph choose to have a right attitude, the right response and move on with this life and not look at what lies behind me, but ahead towards what God has for me.

Joseph was willing to let God's Hand rest upon him no matter what was before him. After Joseph was restored to his family, he told them I know you meant me no harm for it was God who put me here and not you!

To walk in love, the way of forgiveness, to walk in the message of Christ's life, to be a yielded vessel of God and bow our knee to His will for our lives.

This the cross! To see it all as though it was from the Hand of God, for it is!

"PONYTAIL AND A PIZZA"

It is summer now and my girls like I are fish in water, we go as often as possible to swim. The sun is wonderful in its soothing rays and to infiltrate my body with its warmth some how has a healing effect on me.

After this one day of swimming with my girls, Shawna suggests Pizza, of which Trinity quickly agrees to. So off we are to our favorite place, ponytail and all, we will order to go, that way hopefully no one will see me just coming from the pool.

As we waited Shawna says to me, "Mom that guy over there is staring at you"! The two of them quickly talk me out of some quarters for the arcade games as we wait for our order, I just hope it will distract them for the moment. "Mom, Shawna persist, I think he likes you"! I tell her you quit staring at him and ignore him staring at me, he will go away. She teases me as they play the games, he walks over towards the games where we are at, I nervously say "Pizza is ready girls, time to go".

Our pizza is up, they call our number, we get it and head for the door to leave. A couple I know from town stops me to chat a little. The husband says to me, have you noticed that guy over there staring at you Kitty? Yes, I answer! Well he proceeds to tell me he is their friend from San Diego, he is passing through on his way home from a business trip, they stopped in to get some Pizza before he heads home. I think he might like you the guy says to me, he hasn't stopped looking at you the entire time since you walked through that door. Just a little the wife adds! With that I get nervous, saying good-bye and we leave. As we are walking out Shawna says, "told you mom"!

We get home, I shower, pop in my favorite movie, "Wuthering Heights". I get all settled in and the phone rings, it is the couple from the Pizza place. The husband says to me on the phone, "Hey Kitty, look this guy is crazy over you, he is begging us for your number." No! I say to him, I don't know this man. He is a nice guy the couple tell me, he doesn't smoke, drink, take drugs, have a temper, or have child support or alimony coming out of his pocket! I laugh to myself and think well that meets all my requirements. I then ask is he a Christian? Oh yeah the man says! I'm telling you he is a great guy, we have been friends for years, his wife died of Cancer a few years ago, please let us give him your number! No! I tell him again. I hang up telling them I just can't, sorry! I go and finish my movie and go to bed.

The next week-end, the phone rings, it is the wife this time, she says to me, this guy is driving us crazy, just talk to him, please! That's it he just wants to talk with you. We told him you weren't interested, he says to tell you, but he is! That makes me laugh!

Alright! Alright! I now say to her, give him my number, we can talk! That's it! I hang up, not two minutes later the phone rings, it is him! I tell him you sure work fast! He says a guy has to in order for a girl like you not to get away!

I again laugh! He says that's good that I can make you laugh! Look, he says to me, I know you probably have guys falling all over you. I again, laugh! Oh yeah, I think to myself, all over the place. I don't even date! Look he now says to me, let me come up tomorrow, anything you like, the night is yours, you name it!

I tell him wait a minute, I thought you just wanted to talk! I do he says, but while I can see you at the same time! I tell him I don't know you from Adam! He then tells me well you don't know him either, so give me a chance! Dinner! That's it!

Alright! Alright! I now tell him, and he is going crazy on the other end of the phone. I hear a big "YES"! I say to him you are crazy! I just might change my mind! He stops talking and there is dead silence on the other end of the phone. He says you want serious, alright you got serious, I can do that! With the voice of James Cagney! We both crack up at the same time! See you tomorrow night and dinner is on me, we hang up as we tell each other good-night. The phone rings again! It is him! Can I get directions to the place where you want to eat, he says to me? I now am busting up! He says you sure you don't want me to pick you up? No thank you, I'll drive my own car and meet you there!

My girls listened to the entire conversation as they laid next to me on the bed. Yippy! Yippy! Trinity says as she jumps up and down on my bed! Yippy! Mommy is going on a date! Shawna says, "Finally"! In an exhausted tone!

The big day arrives, I get ready and drive to the Restaurant to meet him, he is waiting at the door, and walks me in. I am so nervous, I can feel the heat on my face. He says to me don't be scared I promise to be a gentleman! We go in and sit down to have dinner and visit, the night quickly passes. At the end of the evening he excuses himself to leave for a moment and comes back with two dozen long stemmed soft pink roses. My favorite I think as he hands them to me. I blush!

I've embarrassed you he says, I'm sorry! We continue to visit for some time, having some cheesecake and coffee just to linger the time a little. It is late and time to leave now, we say good-night and I drive home. As I drove home I knew I was in trouble. I already missed him!

I get home take a long hot bath, turn in for the night and fall off right to sleep. I am awaken by the phone ringing, as I reach for it I notice the time on the clock says 3:00 a.m.. It is him, saying just wanted to let you know I got home alright, I knew you wouldn't be able to sleep worrying about my long drive home! I again laugh!

He says is that all you do is laugh? I get silent! No! I answer him, I cry a lot also. What could possibly go wrong in such a pretty lady's life he asks? I am again silent! Don't answer he says, sorry I asked, none of my business.

I tell him maybe another time we could talk, but not now! He is very quiet now and is clumsy with his words, he doesn't know what to say! I feel bad! I think to myself, this guy doesn't have enough time in the day, nor do I care to bother him with it all. He then asks, we still on for next week-end? Yes, I answer! We say good-night and hang-up.

We dated throughout the summer, we all got along just beautifully. My girls couldn't wait for each week-end to come for their time with him. It was as if we had always been, yet two different worlds, and the meeting place was me. I knew my life with him would be completely different than the life I had come from. The times we were together were filled with laughter, a feeling of belonging, of which I had no prior life of. This time, I would think, had to be a complete turn around, I could never live as I had before. At first I even found myself becoming distant from him, almost fearful, evasive, it was all so unknown to me. I didn't know where I was to get the feelings from that I needed, then when they began to surface I hid them. All so complex, new to me, and a journey I had never been on yet longed for. This was to me scary also, but in a new light, inside I knew she was in there, I just had to settle in and let her be the person that was deadened to it all years before.

He was patient with me, he seen through it all, yet never said a word, he just let me learn to relax and not be on the guard all the time, my nature had become defensive. I quickly was brought to a place of letting down my guard and letting him in!

We made plans to remain together, move and settle where he lived, which was fine with me. A new start was much needed and would be so appreciated. A new home, new schools, new surroundings, new faces, of which I did need.

He'd say to me, "you sure you don't want to make this guy happy and elope"? No, I'd laughingly answer! Let's wait until your business trip to San Francisco is behind us, as well as my up-coming court hearings. I needed some space in between to breathe, think and sort it all out. So we waited! Anything you want he'd say to me," the moon is yours, if I could get it down for you I would"!

Maybe next week would be better I would think to myself! I just kept waiting for it all to be right, we had so little time together as it was, I didn't want to spoil this chance!

I was wrong! Next week never came for us. He died that week in San Francisco, a blood-clot had burst in the base of his brain!

This trial would now send me into a two year down hill spin!

“GOING DOWN FAST”

The memories of it all, the years behind me, my life and its cause I now pondered upon. My baby boy, the complications with my girls, the abuse, being in the accident, the $1.00, court, no money, and now this!

Oh I cried! I missed my dear friend of only a few short months, that seemed to come into our lives at a perfect time to rescue my girls and I from it all. Then to be gone when I needed him the most, I became very ill and the stress of it all was taking a toll on me. Again I run for safety!

My refuge awaited me! I cried as He so tenderly picked me up as I fell apart. I would cry out, don’t let me go Lord. For you know you are all I have and I’m putting my trust in you. Hold on to me, as I do to you Lord. God help me!

In my darkest of hours He was there sheltering me from it all. I would try and shut it all out, it wouldn’t go away. Take it from me, please! Oh how I cried for it all to just disappear. I broke and gave him my all. For I couldn’t stop, my body trembled as I layed there. My faced stained with where the tears had fallen, now weak I cry myself to sleep in His loving arms.

I tried to hide it from my girls, for days my mind retraced it all, over and over. I would stand doing dishes staring at the mountains through the kitchen window. My body still weak from the pain, I would again crumble to the floor and weep. I cried, till I could only sob. Saying thank you Lord for him, thank you for the time we did have together. He like you only wanted what was best for me.

Thank you for the little glimmer of happiness you brought me, making me laugh as I so love to do, and once again will.

For days I saw his face, warm, strong, gentle and sensitive. His dark wavy hair, strong arms, and his eyes that would see right through me, I hid nothing from him. Yes, I missed my dear friend, as did my girls as they too retraced funny stories. The time he cooked us spaghetti dinner, putting a towel over his arm, pulling out our chairs and saying, “dinner is served”.

Riding Trinity around on his shoulders, even while he cooked, she would giggle the entire time. He would make excuses to go to the store just so Shawna could buy something. She could talk her way right into his heart and pocket. It was funny to watch them. If I said no! He said we'll see! That remark was a sign to the girls he would talk me into it. The soft pink roses that would adorn my dining table, that he so loved to bring me. All just a part of a memory now.

My body still not fully recovered from my accident. My right foot was now starting to bend to the right, causing me to limp. I would have re-constructive surgery on my foot, of which cost me too for my health insurance was no more either. A cast now on my right foot and up my leg. I once again had to learn to walk all over again. This time hampered for when I got my cast off, my left knee injuries were still not healed. I couldn't put pressure on my right foot, nor on my left leg because of the knee. The torn ligaments would give way, and still needed time to heal, I again revert to crawling on the floor once again. For the weight on either leg sent me to the ground.

Court continued and I only now wanted out from it all, I didn't even want to get out of bed or eat! I needed help in so many ways, with the girls, and after my surgery I couldn't get around, another friend came to the rescue. She is much needed and appreciated. She gets an old steel kitchen chair and puts it in my shower for me, so I can bathe. She wraps a huge lawn bag around my casted leg and gets in with me to wash my hair. It was a funny sight to see.

I was put on pain killers that would put me out for days, many medications I would be allergic to and become extreamly ill. There were days I wouldn't even be able to get out of bed, nor was I coherent. I was allergic to the codeine they gave me for pain, anything in narcotic form sent me spinning for days. At first by it putting me out I was thankful, that way I didn't have to deal, I only wanted the highest cliff to jump from or the deepest river to drown in. By me being on so many drugs it did make it go away some, but then morning always came. The light seemed to find it's way to me, I did prefer it, so I began to fight.

Therapy also continued for me, I remained to limp even worse after my operation. My girlfriend would give me her shoulder and we'd both hobble around my house. I had continuing back problems from the fall. My lower vertabraes were damaged, which in turn caused me neck problems, which in turn made me have migraines that also put me out for days. I had to keep my curtains pulled in my bed-room so not to have extreme pain across my eyes. One day I laughed so hard at it all, I thought surely things can't get any worse! Can they Lord? I again began to laugh hoping not. My girls thought for sure I had went looney from all the medication I was on.

Time again was passing, I was getting stronger yet never really did feel all together, as if I was in a cloud. I got involved with cocaine afterwards and a married man, I thought maybe the two combined would make me forget it all. Neither did, it was all still there the next morning when I awoke, it only made things worse for me inside.

Over the next two years that followed God would heal me physically as well as emotionally and spiritually. My wounds went deep, I had no where to turn but to Him. He was all I had, or could depend upon, and He would prove He was all I needed in a world filled with such pain, isolation, memories and destruction.

I was a mess to say the least. By my running into the arms of another only compounded things for me making it worse. I began to hate it all, I only wanted to retreat, yet that too was not the answer for me. I knew God wanted me to hold still! To pull myself away from all that I surround myself with.

Court continued as did more trials, yet I remained in that safe place I was called to so many times before. The shelter that had proven to always be there for me. He would become my life, my restorer, I so needed Him and He knew I did. It was hard for me to give in, or to give up! I didn't know how! I even needed Him for that, to show me how to surrender to His call. He wanted to take me away, yet my resistance was up, I wasn't sure what to do, or how to do it.

At times my mind only went to retracing the pain of it all. Yet He showed me that too I needed to yield to, good, bad or indifferent, I had to choose to give up. To respond to none of it, but only to Him. He knew all along what I was to do, He allowed me time to see through it all. He patiently held me, and let me kick, scream and resist from within. Knowing the entire time I was going to give up, give in and let it all go. I was to yield to Him and He knew it.

Again what was going to be my response? Now what Kitty? I would drag myself around the house, my knees had calluses on them, dragging my mind also to a place of also wanting to get up! I was determined not to stay down! I would tell myself "Kitty get up!" You are not going to stay down, you will not let this beat you! You will get better!

Sometimes I cried all day, the desperation in me was overwhelming at times, the pain within was compounded with my physical pain. And on top of that my spirit man was slowly fading away. I could feel as the pull was coming from my body and emotions, I was giving way to them. Of which I knew I could not do. But here too I didn't know where to begin, so I fell upon my bed and gave up!

I know no matter how deep our wounds go, they are never beyond the reach of the "Great Physician", he is there ready to heal us. And He awaits us to give in to Him, giving up, to submit, yield to His hand. He then begins the surgery, when we are still before Him. Taking out all that does not belong in us, or that which causes us pain.

Then the sweet healing balm of Gilead is placed on our wounds and there heals us properly to not leave a scar. Amidst it all He always proves Himself strong, He shows Himself to ever be faithful, even when we are not. Through it all I saw that there is a God, it is "HE", that has brought me through, not I nor man!

In this war we are in we must never go, "A.W.O.L.", running from what God wants of us. We are enlisted soldiers, let us prove we are the warriors that our Father has proclaimed us to be! We must get up and begin to take our stand. He has supplied us with everything to fight this fight, and hold our position, not to give any ground up! Not to be moved from our position, no matter what we see or feel, they will only continue to destroy our mission in life. We are asked to do all, and then stand!

Stand means to take or keep your position, to be on our feet, to have a definite opinion, position or attitude, to remain unchanged and to halt and take position for defense or offense, ready to fight! To resist, withstand, endure, to abide by and keep!

This is not a picture of cowards, running from, but to! We are never asked to safely retreat, hide in a fox hole fearing to get our head blown off. Christ as our example never ran from, hid from, He was not moved by what He seen or felt. He only moved in faith that His Father's Will was being performed, this His main concern. As should it be ours as well!

Like Christ, we should now fight the good fight of faith, not to be moved by circumstance, nor be comfortable or complacent. We are being proved, molded, He is making us into His choosing. Never forget we are at War! We are asked to stand, not to retreat! His Image will come forth!

My daughters are raised now and both gone from my home, they too remain to be troopers as well. They know their real home awaits them, never will you hear my girls murmur nor complain, not to believe in the hand of God. They too sheltered from the storms of this life, and both so beautiful to God and I. Their beauty runs deep, they know they are made in the image of, and that love within takes them through till today, as does it I!

"OF THE WRONG COLOR"

The years were quickly passing, I never really dated over the years nor did I ever remarry. God had different plans for me, I would stay busy with helping many children through the years of healing. I had become a Foster Parent for the state of California. I enjoyed children, and it would become a ministry the Lord used for me to get my eyes off of myself and onto those in more need than I.

Getting my eyes off of my circumstances was good medicine, it helped me put my time and energy towards others. It would have been selfish of me to stay all wrapped up in myself, in my own little world, when an extended hand was so needed.

My Lord had done many miracles in my life, in my body and in my heart, it was a healing process of which I owe Him my life, for I had nothing else to give to Him, but me!

Many calls came for children in need, this one day as so many times before, one for a new-born baby girl. Asking if I had room? Yes! Bring her over! My girls and I accepted her with open arms, and soon our hearts were opened up too. She became such a beautiful extension of our home, and a part of our family over the next months that followed. She would be going up for adoption as soon as a bi-racial couple was found for her. Till then we loved her, dressed her up, took her to church, and everyone saw the specialness in her precious little life.

Months passed, another call came, they had found the sister to the baby, now the adoption package changed to a sibling package. A sister, three years old, did I have room? Yes! Bring her over. At the door stood a lovely little girl, with the hugest grin, hair slightly tousled about her head, a smile to brighten any day and eyes of curiosity and questions.

She came in, I introduced her to her sissy, and we all got along beautifully. They were both bright, smart, happy, funny little girls. Which fit perfectly in our home, for my girls were the same. It was fun to watch them together. There was always

“Ding-Dong crumbs on my sofa, loads of clothes to wash, shoes to buckle and smiles to tuck them all in at night”.

Eighteen months now passed, a phone call came, they had found a couple for the girls, my heart sunk. I had them now up to the limit, for now I had a chance to keep them if no one was found to adopt them. Even though the time spent with us brought attachment, bonding and love. I was never considered to be able to keep the girls. For I was told I was the wrong color. There was not a black male presence in our home, our hearts were broken, yet we prepared the girls to leave. I did wonder if the two girls knew the difference, if they saw color, or did they see love. For our love for them was not of any color, it didn’t have a barrier, nor a wall between it. It was simply love that was the bond between us. Only the people making the laws saw it differently, they saw color, they saw a name on a piece of paper that had to be politically correct. That was the saddest thing to tell my girls.

The day arrived, I dressed the girls up for there trip to the park to meet the couple wanting them both. It went well, more visits continued, an over nighter to the couples house. They met their dog, saw their new room, looked at all the new toys and outfits that awaited them. It was perfect!

It all came too soon, the break was harder than the girls and I expected. It took a piece of us that day that we would never be able to reclaim. The couple was so sweet and special to the girls, it made me feel a little more comfortable in letting go. It was time, they were here, parked in the driveway with their new mini-van, were their new mommy and daddy. The back filled with new clothes for the girls, from “Baby By Gosh, Levi, and Carters”. They were off, I bravely buckled them in their new car seats, kissing them fighting back the tears, I didn’t want to cry.

My girls went inside as did I, and cried the day away. Looking at pictures in albums and on the wall, hand prints on Trinity’s mirror, that she refused to wash off, and Shawna sorting through the bows and hair ribbons that she so many times tenderly placed in their hair. Oh mom, they cried, it isn’t fair! I thought to myself as I sat on the floor next to them, your right! It is not fair, but then what is?

Five weeks passed it was going well, we stayed busy and shared of the many memories that we held so dear to our heart. Cooking dinner, I for some reason turn on the T.V. to watch the 4:00 o'clock news, of which I never did. I never had time to sit down with all the kids.

There across the screen came the picture of the little 3 year old girl that had just left our home. I reach to turn it up, the news caster stating she was kidnapped. "Little girl missing from shopping mall", taken while her father shopped.

A command post is set up at the Mall, and police were everywhere combing the area. Also included in on the search "her daddy that just adopted her", he too a police officer.

What I felt in my body was beyond un-belief. Please let this be a mistake, I prayed, let it all be a coincidence Lord. As I continued to listen I soon found out it was no coincidence, it was her.

I go to see them, when I get there, there is T.V. News trucks out front, people all around. I go in we visit and I leave. It all seems so impossible to be happening, everyone is quiet yet friendly.

That evening I call the couple that lived across the street, they now live in Arizona. I tell them about what is going on, they ask Trinity and I to come down for a few days. It is of course wonderful when I get there, she takes me out to eat, takes me shopping and we get ice cream and visit. It is a nice break, the weather is warm, she takes me to drive around town. She even has an older man that she thinks would be good for me, she trys as usual to fix me up! She thinks it's about time I get remarried, she teases and says your not getting any younger, you know! We laugh! No I say to her, and neither is that man!

The phone rings after I'm there for a few days, they need me to come back, the F.B.I. is removing the baby from the couple. They want to place her back with me, can I be there as soon as possible? I leave, the couple drive me the long trip back. I get in my car and now drive to where the baby is, Trinity and I go in, she sees her and goes over immediately and scoops her up, we drive home.

I put her back into the room that she shared with her sissy just five weeks earlier. Trinity can't stand the thought of her being in there all by herself, and asks if she could please come in and share her bedroom with her. I say of course honey, lets move her things over with you. The two got along beautifully, playing the day away as well as the days that followed.

The phone rings the evening after I get her back, it is the adoptive mom, she is sobbing horribly. I try and calm her down, she tells me that she wanted to let me know about it before it hit the News on T.V. Her voice breaking and spurts of words come forth, I start crying just listening to her. She says how her husband confessed of killing the 3 year old, I fall to the floor. Then she tells me last night he had hung himself in her parents garage, she finding him hanging. Everything goes black before my eyes, I listen but hear only an echo. I need a drink of water I try and get up, I can't leave her on the other end. She tells me I know they were your little girls too, you raised them longer than I, I had to tell you, I just couldn't let you hear it on the News. She is consoling me and I her. It is a very painful conversation for the both of us, I remain to sit on the floor. Still listening I cry now, we say good-bye. Oh God! Surround her please with your love!

I turn the News on, it isn't on yet about him, a little time later a News flash comes across the air, it is on him. "Adoptive Dad of said kidnapped little girl is found hanging in garage by his wife."

It has the picture of the house with yellow tape around it posting it as a crime scene. It later tells of his confession, and that they were searching for the remains of the little girl.

The phone rings again, it is the mom, I can't recognize her voice for the sobbing yet I hear her voice breaking as she tries to get out "Kitty"! I say yes!

I too am crying with her, as she says to me, "my entire life is gone, Kitty, in less than one week". I thought as she continued I know, I too have been there. I know also the factor of time and what it holds for us, all can be over in less than a second. My marriage, my two baby girls, our friends, our work together, our life since we were in school. All gone from me! She continues to tell me.

She calms down and asks me how is the baby! I tell her as sweet as ever. Wonder if she remembers me? I tell her I think so, cause she will walk through our home and look in the other rooms as if to look for you. She goes to the front screen door peeks out and claps her hands together for your dog. She is I'm sure missing you too! We again cry.

I ask her, why did they remove the baby from your home, you had nothing to do with what happened. She says, I was no longer a black home, after my husband killed himself! Even though I was white, which they were half of, still it didn't matter. I guess we only got them because of him. And now they are both gone from me, as well as him now too! The air was silent for a while, as I only could listen, the pain was so deep within her, you could hear her heart breaking. I waited for her to calm down and told her that is why I couldn't keep the girls either, they too taken from me cause I was not a black home.

We cry together talk a little more, and say our good-byes and hang-up.

The next afternoon the social worker comes to pick up the baby girl to take her to the Hospital for tests, making sure nothing was done to her. She returned with a rag doll in her arms, a staff member gave it to her to hold as they performed the test. The worker begins to tell me she was fine except that the D.N.A. testing showed she was not sharing the same biological father with her sister as thought. In fact there was a question if she was even the same racial make-up, they were unsure.

My head was spinning now, she was only a name on a piece of paper, caught in a system of being politically correct. And we are told all done for the best interest of the children.... Oh God, I cried inside what was this all for?

I now again ask to keep her, and told considering the special circumstances it was probable. I was excited, I wanted her so, I had her as a new-born. Now some 20 months later and all this behind us, I know I am the one to have her, her little innocent life needed to stay with my girls and I.

The phone rings weeks later, she now tells me we have found another home for the baby. Another couple wants to adopt her, the same make-up as before. I am dumbfounded to say the least. I hang up and cry, they told me if it was too hard for me to let her go, they would remove her from me. Letting her stay with another Foster Family until the adoption was completed. No! I said, I can do it!

I call everyone, anyone, someone! Please listen! I have had this baby for over 18 months, let me keep her, why does she need to leave my home. You don't need to find a home to adopt her, I want her. All the doors were closed, it was priority for them to match with the racial make-up of the child. But she is half of what I am, and I already love her. The adoption will go forth as planned, I'm told.

I sit down that evening to watch the follow up on the story, continuing to carry the news. Telling of his confession, how he did it to her, and of him killing himself.

"The 3 year old was dismembered, and then incased in cement, then he scattered her body parts throughout the county."

Oh God! I fell apart just to think of it, over and over it continued to play in my head.

I now shut it off, I try to tune it out, my heart was so heavy.

The call comes, they have a family and will start the process all over. Repeating itself, my girls and I go through the steps all over again, painful yes, but we were the one's to do it. She needed us to be strong for her, she didn't understand why I was to give her away again. Her innocent eyes caught mine and said it all, I will never forget that look. So full of questions, so many answers un-spoken to her, she was feeling shuffled, and not wanted. How could I tell her how much I wanted her, what I had done to keep her. I never wanted her to leave us. So many words to say, yet not enough to make it right! So I kept silent!

My girls and I go through the motions again, we have no peace with this. The pain too deep this time, my girls dress her and kiss her good-bye and have to leave. Unable to watch her go again, they go with their arms tearing away from her. My girls too would like her carry the scars of that day forever in their hearts. I finish packing her things, smelling them, trying to hold on to even the sweet scent she would leave. Telling her as she sat there helping me, I will never fold your clothes again baby. I will never tuck you in, nor will I get to have food fights with you. Or chase you through the house when you escape from your bath, no more Ding Dong crumbs in my sofa, no more chocolate milk kisses at lunch time. She so sweetly listens as I talk to her as I finish up getting her ready to go.

The time comes for her to go from me once again, she will leave from the office this time, and not from my home. We take the drive together, she looks adorable, in her little levi out-fit, with a lavender ribbon tied in her hair.

I take her in, smiling on the outside, I sit her down. The worker comes over to take her, I bend down and kiss her soft little precious cheek, whispering I love you baby girl. I leave!

I again drive home alone, the feelings that surround me are familiar ones, I am getting used to them. These past years have broke me in. My arms empty, I go in my house. Sitting on my bed I reach for her little rag doll that I kept from when she went for her tests. It has her little sub-bonnet on it's head from when she was a new-born. I hold it and cry, I sit it down back in the whicker basket next to the bear from some twenty years earlier. They remain sitting next to each other all now a memory, yet one day we will all be united.

The following week the 3 year olds funeral was held in town, her birth parents attending, they lived in the same town as I. News cameras everywhere, I stand off to the side alone. Her tiny white casket, adorned with flowers atop, and a carved lamb in the headstone. There were people there that had only heard of what had happened to her from the News. Not knowing her or her baby sister now adopted again. Her birth mother comes over to me, we hug. She tells me Kitty you should have been able to keep my two girls, I wanted you to have them. The Grand-mother comes over as well, we embrace, I made her a special frame of pictures of her grand-daughter that was killed. She asks me of the baby, did you get her back? Are you able to keep her now? Do you think we can see her again? I fight back the tears.

I tell her no! She was adopted again. Oh No! She states. I take a single soft pink long stemmed rose and lay it across her tiny casket. I leave.

I drive away alone, the stereo on, the air in my face calms me. I drive around for awhile before going home. We talk once again.

Lord! I am not going from your side, no matter what I see or feel! I will stand! Help me Lord! Help me see my way through all of this! I know you have a purpose for everything, I won't question you! Just don't leave me alone in all of it!

"If only for the time you had them, it was for you to just love them. If only for a second, just to be there. If only for then, it was for now!"

He always reminded me of....Himself. He too alone! He too wanting a family! He too! Like us! Created in His Image! We too, share with Him, all that He is!

What He did then for us, was for now. The time then! For Him to share His Love with us. The second of time that passed as He gave the life of His only begotten Son, for us!

Who was I to complain? Who was I to ask why? Who was I to think I was alone in all this? I too must not only share in His blessings but also partake of His sufferings. Who was I? Was I above it all? Did I think I was too good for such things to happen to me?

Oh Lord! Forgive me! I don't want to put myself above you, you too have hurt! You too alone! You too have given much up! You too made sacrifices! You too want to be loved! I now see your heart in it all. I will stand and only do as you will in my life. Take me to that place where you have wanted me to go, I will follow.

“TO HIM BE THE GLORY”

“Seek the Lord and His
strength, seek His…
presence continually.”

1 Chronicles 16:11

"JESUS"
"GOD'S ARMOR"

I do not tell you of my life to bring light to myself, but to shed light on God. And Him for taking me through it all, it is clear to me that satan has wanted my life for some time now. I know I pose a threat to the enemy's camp!

I say "Praise God"! It is time to buckle up, stand firm, and press on! To be strong in the Lord and in the strength of His power. Putting on the "whole armor of God". So that you may be able to stand against the wiles of the devil.

For our struggle is not against enemies of flesh and blood, but against the rulers, against the authorities, against cosmic powers of this present darkness, against the forces of the "evil one", in the heavenly places.

Therefore take up the whole armor of God, so that you may be able to withstand on that day of evil, and having done all, "to stand firm". Stand therefore and fasten the belt of truth around your waist, put on the breastplate of righteousness, as shoes put on the gospel of peace. Therefore, take the shield of faith to be able to quench "all", the flaming arrows of the evil one.

Take the helmet of salvation, and the sword of the Spirit, which is the Word of God. [Ephesians 6:10-16]

Here let me note a key point as well as a key word. It is "God's", armor, not ours. It does not and will not fit as we remain in the world, or its ways. Nor if we are being used by the enemy against one another in the Body. The armor of God will never fit you or I in a state of flesh, we must fit into Him first.

We must fit into Him to be able to wear it, we must put on the Lord Jesus Christ! [Romans 13:14] Put on the Lord Jesus Christ, and make "no" provision for the flesh, to gratify its desires. In verse 12, it states, "put on the armor of light."

Putting Him on, is putting on the armor, He is our armor of light! He is our armor of God!

The armor of God does not come in different colors of our choosing, it is not made to order, nor to our form, it is God's not ours. It does not wait for us to put it on each morning, nor does it sit at the foot of our bed waiting for us to remember it. We had better not have it off! For if we are out of Christ, out of the attributes of Christ, not fitting into His character. We are in deep trouble!

Do not treat it as a light matter, nor with folly! Our stand is "in" Him. For in this life we now lead, we battle against, "rulers and authorities", [the powerful evil forces of fallen angels headed by satan, who is a vicious fighter].

1st Peter 5:8 tells us to discipline ourselves, keep alert. Like a roaring lion your enemy, and your adversary the devil is prowling around, looking for someone to devour.

Devour means to eat up greedily, to eat away at, consume, or to destroy.

To withstand these attacks we must depend wholly upon God's strength and use every piece of His armor. It is not a mere fantasy, satan and all his demons are real, and out there. We face them everyday, some more than others, it all depends on how much of a threat you pose to his camp. You belong to Him, to Christ?

Guess what? The devil is your enemy! Or at least suppose to be! He will do and try everything he can get away with to destroy us, to divert our attention away from Christ and back onto him and the world. All to keep us from our mission down here, getting our eyes off Christ and on the problem. Let us be strong in the Lord and in, the strength of His might! [Ephesians 6:10]

Yes! We are a victorious army, yet we must engage in the struggles of this life here, on the battlefield of trials, until Christ's return. God has given power to us to win! The Holy Spirit within us, and His Armor [Jesus], surrounds us.

"On this rock I will build my church, and the gates of hell "will not" prevail against us. [Matthew 16:18]

The rock, [Jesus], the church, [us], the substance holding it all together is love, the hand of God. It is He who is our sustainer, He the holder of our life.

Therefore "love does no wrong to a neighbor; love therefore is the fulfillment of the law. And this do, knowing the time, that it is already the hour for you to awaken from sleep; for now salvation is nearer to us than when we believed. The night is almost gone, and the day is at hand. Let us therefore lay aside the deeds of darkness and put on the "ARMOR OF LIGHT". [Romans 13:10-12]

Do we see what the armor is? The armor of God, is the armor of light! Jesus!

Armor is a covering worn when fighting, to protect the body! That's us! Our armor to protect us the body is the Son of God, Jesus! We put Him on! We are remember hidden in Christ, as the word tells us.

We must clothe ourselves in Him, in Truth, standing in His righteousness, spreading the good news, to walk in faith, be saved, use the word. This ensures us to be able to quench the flaming darts of the enemy. This is what we the church must be clothed in, these attributes of Christ. It is nothing in ourselves that we fight this fight we are in. It is all contained in Him.

The armor contains the "Belt of Truth", know satan's lies and remain firm in who you listen to. [God's truth or the devil's lies, your choice].

The "Breastplate of Righteousness", this covers who we are "in", Christ Jesus, our right standing is in Him, not in ourselves.

The "Shoes", are ours in the readiness to spread the good news, which is that we have access to God, through His Son, Christ Jesus. Our hearts should be as His, "no not one should parish, no not one".

The "Shield of Faith", is the opposite of what satan wants us to do, which is to doubt God's Word. The Word of God, is Jesus! The word became flesh and dwelt among us!

The "Helmet of Salvation", is in what God did when He came and gave Himself up to die on the cross, God, in the very presence of His only begotten Son. We must believe this to be saved, this is our helmet to protect our minds.

The "Sword of the Spirit", is in what God's word tells us, and is our only weapon of offence in our battles we wage against the enemy. The Spirit of God lives within us now, He is our Teacher to War!

After we have done everything, to "Stand Firm". [Ephesians 6:13]

We must stand in Christ to remain in God's Armor! In the flesh! You are in "BIG TROUBLE". See the enemy knows if he can get you out from this armor, your position, of who you are "in", Christ Jesus, he has us defeated. Yet we must believe God's word, for it tells us that satan has already been defeated! Amen!

No matter our circumstances, the victory is ours, contained in the truth of the word, Jesus! He said it, that settles it, no and's, if's or but's about it. We are victorious in the stand we take in Christ Jesus, in Him, not ourselves.

Remember always His promises to us, He will keep them. Man will fail us, God will never fail us. He is ever faithful to us, leaving us never to be alone.

We are enlisted soldiers, drafted upon our recruitment into His family, the army of God. We must begin to now stand up and fight......Fasten down the helmet, slip into the shoes, keeping our sword drawn at all times. Never go anywhere without your sword. The sword is His word "JESUS", he is alive in our lives.

God's armor will see us through, it is ours to remain in, if we remain in Christ. The armor is that light that will shine upon, and through all darkness.

Therefore we need not move outside of His armor, no matter what it look's like, go on God's Word, not on what you feel or see. Both sight and feelings are remember dangerous, meant to defeat us, pull us under, to devour.

God says to stand for a reason, for if you are caught off guard sitting down on the job, or laying down reclining. You will be off guard! We must remain to stand.

We must keep our position that Christ left for us until His return. Not to budge or give an inch of land back that He died for. He knew what we would be facing, He faced it before us. He knew what we would need to fight, stand and win for He supply's all our needs, according to His riches and glory.

You know as well as I, what is out there. I have felt much and seen much, yet while in the trenches of this life, yes wounded, but not mortally. I will continue to stand up for what He stood for, to press on for my Lord. He is worth all to me.

His strength provides all we need, it is not us that contain anything within ourselves that will see us through. It is in God alone and in His powerful presence within us that contains all we need.

"Anything worth something, will always be costly". God knew this and that is why He had the ultimate price paid for us by His only begotten Son, in giving His very life so that we might have life.

Will you and I now pay the price, is it worth it to us, will we now die to ourselves so that His life can then move through us? To a needy world full of pain, death, destruction, lies, is it worth it to us church? I say "Yes"!

We are now the hands, feet, words, and love extended to others by the Lord. He has done all that He is going to do, He is not ever going to leave His throne, come here and die again. As He said on the cross, "it is finished".

The Father's Will, fulfilled in and through His son's death on the cross, once and for all! All that will now call upon His name and trust Him alone.

Looking to no other for your need, nor your reward. Looking nowhere except into the eyes of Jesus, the eyes that saved you and I. He alone hears yours cries, your pleas for help, our very heart beat is felt by Him, it is His! Our breath! His! We should never use our trials for defeat or for a cause of question of God's hand upon our lives.

How can we the "Body of Christ" continue on like this? We know what the truth is, it is in God's word, and we know who lives in us, God the Holy Spirit.

For if the Spirit of Him who raised Jesus from the dead dwells within you, He who raised Christ from the dead will give life to your mortel bodies also through His Spirit that dwells "in you". [Romans 8:11]

Or do you not know that your body is the "temple of the Holy Spirit" who is in you, which you have from God, and that you are not your own? [1 Corinthians 6:19]

We are not alive anymore! Why do we care to carry dead bones around with us? Do we like the stench of rotting flesh? When our flesh rises up to relive to have it's own way! Remind it, it is dead! Read the word to it! Speak the word to those dead bones of yours and get a shovel and go to the cemetary and bury him under the blood. Your either alive or dead, how can something dead have it's own way? Or tell us what it wants? It can't that's the point! So if we are dead and it is no longer us that lives but Christ, that now lives in us. What are we doing? Either God's word is the truth and the devil is a liar, and we start acting like it. Or we have made no difference. We are just dead bones walking!

We are told to be strong in the Lord and in the strength of His power. It is not us, we can not do a thing aside from our Father giving it to us. It is all done completely for us by Him.

He supply's all our needs, His love is even proven to us by His armor supplied to us. He knew we wouldn't be able to do it on our own, so He again gave of Himself, to us. He gives us everything to fight this fight we fight.

We are told in His word that our fight is not against flesh and blood, it is against satan. I know my fight was not with my husband, my love for my husband was standing. I had done all as God say's and then I stood. The ground was not lost, the battle belonged to the Lord. He was not defeated in my life. He always proved Himself strong, especially since I knew I was weak. This gave Him the ability to move in and fight for me! I stood! I was not going to look at it in the flesh, I had to go by faith.

The assurance of a promise to me from God is worth me standing on, my husband did not lose his salvation, he is with our Lord. For nothing remember can separate us from the love of God, He is ever faithful and with us. One person is not worse than thee other, we are all equally wrong, one sin is not greater than another. It is up to God not us, we can never weigh someone's salvation, it is not in us being good. It is in Christ Jesus and what He did.

For there is no distinction, since "all" have sinned and fall short of the glory of God; they are now justified by" His grace as a gift", through the redemption that is "in", Christ Jesus, whom God put forward as a sacrifice of atonement by "His blood", made effective through "faith". He did this to show "His righteousness", because in His divine forbearance He had passed over the sins previously committed, it was to prove at the present time that He, Himself is righteous and that "He", justifies the one who has faith in Jesus. (Romans 3:22-26)

"Jesus"
"God's Truth"

Again, it is He, not us. He has done this for us. Rather it be murder or doubt, it is all sin, everything ever done is capable by all. Sin is sin! Anything even imagined is sin. You do not need to put your hand to someone to kill them. Just not forgive, be angry, think ill of them, or speak ill of them, the thought is just as well a sin. There is the tongue, a wicked piece of the body, if not controlled holds the very power of life and death. (Proverb 18:21)

One factor to check ourselves on to see if we are living by the Holy Spirit's power, is self control. It is a piece of the fruit we bear forth if he is in control of our life. It is singular, "Fruit", it is not fruits. It is a part of His work in us, they are the by-products of Christ's life, we are to submit to Him to be able to produce a productive life. This again not done by us, it is He that grows within us, to bring us to a point of growth in Him.

His love thought of it all, he knew this, and that is why it is supplied to us His children. We simply slip into Him, that is a wonderful place to be, hidden in Christ. It is here that His production takes place, as well as His protection.

See God knew my heart, as well as my husbands. God judges the heart of man, man judges the outside. He knew I loved my husband, no matter what I seen in the natural, I stood on God's word that He would be there for me.

See the power of God will take us through, we have no power in ourselves outside of our heavenly Father giving it to us. For the same power contained in the "Creation", by the Holy Spirit.

The same power contained in the "Parting of the Red Sea", by the power of God, the Holy Spirit.

The same power contained and spoken into a "Virgin Girl", and the spoken word became flesh and dwelt among us, by the Holy Spirit.

The same power of the Holy Spirit that raised the dead, healed the lame, opened blind eyes, spoke to the possessed, and they were delivered.

The same power that was in the "Resurrection", and this same power that now lives within you and I, is the power that is going to take us to meet Christ, in the clouds. To be with our Father, to unit us as the "Bride", to "Him", the Son of God, for the wedding of all weddings!

What is wrong with us? That same powerful presence of God, the precious Holy Spirit now lives in us, church!

Oh Father, forgive us for we know not what we have done! We have yet to see the Holy Spirit released or poured out as spoken of, because of how we continue to remain. In our attitudes of self-righteousness, our haughty eyes, continuing to speak ill of each other. To be selfish with ourselves and our time, we have come to a place of thinking we are really it! When really we are suppose to not be it! He must now be it, and that is all going to be! For we have not become thee extended hand of Christ as the Father has so purposed.

Never should we have begun to listen to satan's lie and remain a part of his useless ugly life, full of petty games played against one another. It is simple again, you are either serving God, or you are not! And if not, then who? If not God and His ways and will, then it is another!

Do we read the Word church? Do we? Then why have we been listening to a defeated foe? Why have we played right into his hands?

The proof is in the pudding! We had best begin to believe the truth, and not buy into a lie anymore.

For we are more than conquerors through Christ who strengthens us, great are our weapons for pulling down strongholds, greater is "He" that lives within us, than he that lives in the world. No weapon that is fashioned against us shall prosper, we are an heir of God and a joint heir with Jesus Christ. A chosen generation, a royal priesthood, a holy nation, God's child. There is no condemnation for those "in" Christ Jesus.

If God is for me, who can be against me? I can be and do all things in Christ who strengthens me, one thing I do: forgetting what lies behind and straining forward to what lies ahead. I press on to the goal for the prize of the upward call of God in Christ Jesus, my Lord.

I am not luke warm, I will win, I am an overcomer, I will not compromise. For the Spirit of the Lord is upon me, anointing me to preach good news to the poor. To proclaim release to the captives, to recover sight to the blind, giving liberty to those oppressed, and to bind up the broken-hearted. To proclaim the acceptable year of the Lord.

I will be anxious for nothing, for truly the "Joy of the Lord is my Strength". Lord grant to me your servant to speak your word with all boldness while you stretch out your hand to heal, and signs and wonders are performed through the "name of Jesus".

These are just some of God's words to us church! It is our sword! We should begin to believe it, read it, use it, live it, become it! It is who we are "in", Christ Jesus! We can live our very lives upon His word, it will never steer us wrong, nor leave us, betray us, abandon us. He is our very strength to continue on in! His life is now our life!

This is who we are! God has spoken! He can not lie! We must begin to build our self worth upon "Him".

For if you are out there trying to build self up, looking to build your own self worth up, you are still alive!

If it is important to you to build up your self esteem or someone else's, you are still alive, and better check for a heartbeat, (spiritually that is). If you find one you better get out your shovel and go back to the cemetery and bury those dead bones. It is works on our part, we should have no self-esteem, for our self died didn't it? Or are you still trying to keep it alive? God can not Lie! Nor will He! He is God, He is a man about His word, we are suppose to be dead church! He is who must live, not us and our life.

We are suppose to be born-again, this means our old self is dead and so must our ways to self be, "dead"! If we continue to be today as we were then! To be treating others as before, feeling superior to others! Having an attitude of self righteousness, remaining in manipulation, control of others, rudeness, cold. To be so full of ourselves that we have left Jesus out! Have we become above it all?

You had better be checking for a heartbeat, if it beats to to any of the above. Guess what? Yep, you're still alive. Only

Christ should be seen now, to exist, only His life through us. The example of Christ and His life as seen through our life to others!

It is remember now Christ and His life that should live in and through us. Who are we to be concerned with ourselves at a time like this anyway? God our Father has waited for this moment in our life time, (for God lives outside of time), for us, His children alive today to realize this. What He has done for us, those who believe in Him and trust in all His ways. No matter what! These are the ones He will rise up to do His work in these last days.

To follow the leading of the Holy Spirit within us, continue in God's word, which is the life of Christ!

"Jesus"
"God's Body"

We must crucify the flesh, "For those who belong to Christ "Have", crucified the flesh with it's passions and desires. If we live by the Spirit, let us also be now guided by the Spirit.

Let us not become conceited, competing against one another or envying one another." (Galatians 5:24-26)

"Have" means to be done on our part in an action. Have is meaning to cause to do or to be done, this is our's to do. These desires do not always have to be carnal, they can be ambition anger, envy, conceit, pride, lust, possessions, jealousy, or to live a certain lifestyle. By crucifying these and others in our life we can then be transformed into the image of Christ and be and do the Will of our Father.

For by grace you have been saved through faith, and this not on your own doing, it is a gift of God not the results of works, so that anyone may boast. For we are what He (GOD), has made us, created "in", Christ Jesus for good works, which God prepared beforehand to be "our way of life." (Ephesians 2:8-10)

We can never work our way to Heaven, it is not contained in anything you could ever do, it is a gift. Out of our gratitude to God, then we should seek to help and serve others with, kindness, charity, and love. To love the brethren leads us to a life filled with God's approval and above all to love Him above all others.

He continues to give us gifts, to help us as a church, God never meant it to be run by one man. The gifts are put into what we call the "Five Fold Ministry", or the "Hand of God", as a working unit they can administer God's equipping of the saints. "The gifts He gives were that some would be apostles, some prophets, some evangelists, some pastors and teachers, to equip the saints for the work of the ministry, for "building up the body of Christ", until "all", of us come to the unity of the faith and knowledge of the Son of God, to the maturity and the full statue of Christ.

We must no longer be children, tossed to and fro and blown about by every wind of doctrine, by people's trickery, by their craftiness in deceitful scheming. But speaking the truth in love, we must "grow up in every way into Him who is the head, into Christ", from whom the "whole body", joined and knit together by "every ligament", promoting the "body's growth in building itself up into love". (Ephesians 4:11-16)

Apostles, Prophets, Evangelists, Pastors, Teachers, these are all to equip the saints for the work of the ministry. All are needed, it is proven here in Gods word. All these ministries are about to be put into full use, for the body truly needs to be built up! Amen? For our unity of the faith and for the knowledge of the Son of God.

These are a working unit, not one. But all! All five! For the good of the brethren, so that we will grow properly and promote the growth of the body, (you and I), in building itself "up" in love.

So that all the members are placed where they can be used as so purposed, just as in our natural body. Each member has a particular use and function, so is it as well with our spiritual body. This is all done so that we as the Body of Christ can move and function as we were so purposed to do by the Father.

Remembering it is the entire body, not a hand, not a nose, not a eye, not a foot, we all have purpose, a function. God gives this membership placement to the body, it is proven not everyone is in their rightful place as yet. Other wise we would be moving forward and proclaiming to all God's Will.

When God's order is in place, we will see the church move as so purposed and ordered and set down by God "not man"! This is the gift given to the "Fivefold Ministry", to in turn give back unto us the body.

God gives this wisdom and knowledge to the Apostles and the Prophets, to impart to others their call from God. This is not the job of the Pastor, Teacher, or Evangelist, they shepard, teach and preach the gospel.

Neither is one person the body, they do not hold all the positions of God's calling. If you have one person that is doing the ministries of other members, this does not mean that one does not have place or use within the body. Nor does it mean this one person is called to these ministries by God, but by man or themselves. It might be a spirit of pride, control or a jezebel spirit dominating not only at home but as well on Sunday. This is why the "Fivefold Ministry" is also needed, God will tell them who needs to be where and who doesn't.

Such has gone on within the body that has been ruled by satan, and not by God, works of the flesh given over to such disorder.

Still we must continue on to what we are purposed for, no matter what has happened to us, in or out of the church. No matter what has been done to us, (even ones in the church), pay them no mind, only focus upon Jesus. Know that our Heavenly Father has seen it all, He is the one to give back what they have given.

If one has done these things and continue on in the church, in the ways of the flesh and not of the Spirit. Again be aware! For the separation has begun, between the sheep and the goats. (And as Keith Green sang in one of his songs, the only difference between the two, is what you did and didn't do!)

Hold on to your hats, for many of us will be surprised when it is apparent of who has grown up between us. Looking like the real thing, but it is not! Satan is a deceiver, a counterfeiter, just like phony bills are passed off. They are not genuine, they are false, a fake, a false imitation of the real thing. Looks like! Talks like! Walks like! But! It is not like! It is a look alike, very close to the real thing, very similar to. But remember satan's job is to deceive us, that is his biggest weapon. He is a liar, and we best not buy his goods any longer, he has gotten away with this for too long.

But when the light is held up to a counterfeit it will fail the test, no longer able to be passed off any longer as the real thing. The deceit will be found out, a counterfeit all this time passed off as the real thing to us. But the "light of Christ" will unveil, revealing one's true face. We need to start looking at ourselves in the mirror now, while we have time. Repent from all, and never put our hand to such again! For counterfeits are copied to look like as to pass off as! But not for long! For God's voice is about to be made known.

Here we know they will be able to mingle among us, look like, and to have the appearance of, yet on that day many will say, "Lord, Lord, didn't I?" Only to be told to depart from me, for I, (God), never knew you! God's love will prevail, it will win over. It is the force of which will expose all, for it will bring light to that which has been hidden in the darkness. Love!

God's love for us is His very presence of His word, of which is Jesus! He is the visible light of who God is. Are we like Christ? Do we do as He did? Do we go about doing good as He? Or are we doing good as in a state of how we are? Big difference church! One is selfless, the other selfish! Are we doing good? Or are we doing good? Which is it?

Let us pray we will make a difference church. For our very prayer life should be a lifestyle, not just mere words. Our lives should offer up our prayers as we walk in the Spirit! In God's ways and remain in Christ Jesus, as an ever sweet smell unto His nostrils. It is not ten minutes here or there, time that we have sat aside throughout our busy day! In the middle of our daily schedule's of what we do!

Again, who are we? Who are we to put God on hold, until we have time, or we are ready! To our beckon call, when we have the time for Him! How selfish of us to think as this. Who are we but dust!

We make our very life as a prayer, it is constantly responding to God's life in us. It is a lifestyle not time set aside. How in the world can we expect to hear His voice when we are only listening on our terms? He always desires to talk with us, He just needs to know we want Him to! Or are we always saying something? Can we not be still and know that He is God! Listen for the small, still quiet voice from within! We ramble on, and don't give Him time to be heard!

Does anyone do this to you? Does it not make you shy away? Does it not make you feel unimportant? As if they are the only one's that need to be heard? Let us not make this same mistake with Him.

"Pray in the Spirit at all times, in every prayer and supplications" (Eph. 6:18)

In the Spirit, how can we not! He lives within us. We are, or should be in constant contact with "Him". Our prayer life is an extension of our relationship with our Lord. It is not merely a word, but an attitude revealed in an action. It is not only a verbal expression of our needs and wants. It is spiritually contained within us, ever to be lifted up!

We must not only talk the talk, but we must walk the walk! Amen! For the love shown to us by the Father who so loved us that "He gave", this is not in a mere word. But an attitude revealed to us in an action! And the same is expected of us, "For by this everyone will know you are Christ's disciple, "if" we have love for one another. (John 13:35)

The word "if", here is used as a choice word on our part, if we choose. If we do, then we are. It is an action, not a word, this life of ours. Never did Christ say, "I Love You". He proved it to us with His very actions upon the cross.

Again revealed in an action, both from God the Father, as He gave. And also as God the Son, as He gave. And now we have God the Holy Spirit within us, and He too is ready to give. Remembering that we are the house of God, we are His Temple, we are His dwelling place, we now the Body of Christ here on earth holds His Presence.

Do you not know that you are the temple of God, and that the Spirit of God dwells in you? (1st Corinthians 3:16) Or do you not know that your body is a temple of the Holy Spirit who is in you, whom you have from God, and that you are not your own? (1st Cor. 6:19) So then you are no longer strangers and aliens, but you are fellow citizens with the saints, and are of God's household, having been built upon the foundation of the Apostles and Prophets, Christ Jesus Himself being the corner stone, in whom the whole building, being fitted together is growing into a holy temple in the Lord; in whom you also are being built together for a habitation of God in the Spirit. (Ephesians 2:19-22) For a habitation "OF GOD" in the "SPIRIT"! We! His dwelling place! He wants to live in us! Me and you!

God's very presence of who He is, is proof to us, in God the Father, God the Son, and God the Holy Spirit, "He is God". A real person, but He is also God. For there is one body and one Spirit just as also you were called in one hope of your calling; one Lord, one faith, one baptism, one God and Father of all who is over all and through all and in all. (Ephesians 4:4-6)

He has proven His love to us and remains to do so till today. For His person is not only triune, His love not only triune, but His existence is also. God in three persons, yet one. Having a three part existence! He is the glory in the church and by Christ Jesus to all throughout all ages, world without end. Amen. (Ephesians 3:21)

For in the Old Testament it is He, God the Father that is revealed, in the New Testament it is He, God the Son that is revealed, and now it is He, God the Holy Spirit that is about to be revealed, to us church! For they are one! He is God! Amen!

God wanted to be loved, accepted, then as now. For He is "God the same yesterday, today and forever." (Hebrews 13:8) Yet in the Old Testament God the Father, "rejected", in the New Testament God the Son, "rejected"! Now with us, God the Holy Spirit. And now its up to us church! What are we going to do with Him? God!

God is waiting for His last chapter in His word to be fulfilled.

"Behold, I stand at the door and knock. If anyone hears My voice and opens the door, I will come "in to him" and dine with him, and he with me.

To the one who conquers I will give a place with me on my throne." This is in (Revelation 3:20-21), and church this is for today! He is knocking upon the doors of our hearts, are we too going to turn Him away?

Yes! Church it is up to us now, if we so choose, it is God the Holy Spirit, here with us today revealing Himself so that we might conquer. What are we going to do? Are we too going to reject Him? The very presence of God! Like the men of old? No! Not unless you want to sit where I want to sit, a place awaits all who conquer, it is His word. Ours through our obedience, then as now. Obedience is what He wants from us, if we want to, not because we are made to.

He continues to knock upon our hearts church, to take away the stones of hardness and replace with a heart of flesh, moldable and touched by His Hand! It is not too late, He wants to be asked in. In our hearts, our lives, our future, He desires all that you desire.

For our life now contains His desires, and our lives are His desire.

"Jesus"
"God's Love"

He wants fellowship, He is a gentle-man, He will wait until we open our hearts to Him, our door. He will never force Himself upon us, nor make us do anything we do not want to do. He wants for us to choose, our choice "if", we take that step or not!

But I wouldn't wait too long if I were you, we are never assured of having tomorrow, plus the hand extended to us now is that of grace, but it won't be for long.

If you are a Christian and not yet filled with the life and power of God's presence, the Holy Spirit. The Spirit's power is contained within us! He is not going to come down out of the sky in some mystical way. He is within us, therefore He will move in and through us. Baby get filled to the brim, for it's about time to cross over into that promised land. Spiritually of what awaits us is beyond anything touched upon as yet. It too promised to us in the word, so get ready!

He desires for us to have what is best for us, you and I. That is to do the will of the Father, moving in the power of the Holy Spirit, so that the life of Christ can be revealed to all. It is going to be an exciting time, for He is about to be poured out, of us, who so choose to be broken vessels. Not caring to remain the same, nor will the world remain the same after we the church submit to the gentle hand of our Father.

We need the Holy Spirit church. We can not fool ourselves nor are we fooling the world, they too know if we have the goods or not. They are watching us! He is the force that will lead us up and out of this mess we have only made for ourselves. All because we have listened to a liar, (satan), instead of the truth, (Jesus). Don't forget he is defeated, by the blood of the Lamb and the word of our testimony. And believe me satan hates both! The blood and we too for telling what it has done for us, and proclaiming to all.

The (Blood), is an extremely powerful thing, I did a study on the blood, and during it God said look it up! I did!

“Blood”- the dark red liquid that is pumped by the “Heart”, to every part of the “Body”, bringing “Oxygen”, and digested “Food”, carrying waste material away from it.

It’s us I thought! OH! It is God the Father as the “Heart”, pumping this blood to us the “Body”, bringing “Oxygen”, (the Holy Spirit), who is our breath of life. And digesting the “Food”, (Jesus) who is our bread of life. And all waste material is carried away by it the Blood. The blood carries away all that is not good for us, the junk in the body is not allowed to remain, it is. The breath of life, the bread of life, for our life!

It is all contained in the “BLOOD,” spiritually as well as physically, either way it cleanses and brings life. It is here that our life flows into His and His into ours. The Blood, how it cleanses us from sin. From life giving to cleansing, it is powerful and needed, in both.

The “Blood”, Oh church! What a life giving force it is, and forever bringing life to us in both our lives. We should be so very grateful, humble and submitting ourselves at the feet of Him who saved us from it all. The “Blood” our rescuer as well as our restorer, at His feet to remain there until He is finished with us. Trust Him church! We will come out as so purposed, of use, just as was the Son.

We must remain in Christ Jesus, knowing who He is, and what He did for us in the shedding of His blood. Stand firm in who we are in Him, looking at His death and what it really did for us. We the body of Christ.

We must no matter what allow our life to now become an expression of Christ and His life, as in (Galatians 2:20) I have been crucified with Christ, never the less I live; yet not I, but Christ lives in me; and the life I now live in the flesh, I live by the faith of the son of God, who loved me and gave His life for me. (Have been here indicates again already done, passed tense!)

Our ministry is contained within what He did for us and not what we do for Him, through the life of Christ, not us! We are only thee extension of that life. It is not contained within the four walls where we go to on a Sunday morning, this is not the church! That building is not the church until we step into it, we are the church. We are to be built up not those four walls, we are His dwelling place, not those four walls, we are the building of God. We enter His gates with thanksgiving and praises from within, we enter into His courts with a humble heart, that now reveals His life!

We are to lay our lives aside and now live as Christ did, die to self and only now give ourselves to others as did He. To serve, to be that living sacrifice now and lay it all at the altar, at the feet of Him who raised us up with Him. This is again not contained between the four walls on a Sunday morning, it is a life-style. Don't be fooled into serving a dead religion, for we serve a live God.

It is this love that we now contain within us that is to be revealed, as did our example set before us, Christ Jesus. So must we now in submission, being only obedient to our Father.

For Jesus not only commands love, but He himself practiced it. It is not merely His thoughts but His will, but above all His deeds. If our love is real it will be expressed as well as was Christ's. For Jesus left no doubt in people's lives, they knew He cared. His caring touched others lives and made a difference, as should ours today. Can we say the same church? Have we touched others as Christ? Or have we been used as a tool of satan pitted against one another? Bringing harm, pain, rejection, to those within the body?

God now dwells in us, so we are now "His Body", He desires to express His love, His very self now though us. In this love we should never only love others because we want their love or something in return, instead we should be loving others because we are loved by God. He wants us to do more than to drift through life, He wants us to be an influence for Him. And an extension of His outstretched hand of love to a dying and needy world.

To bear one another's burdens and thus fulfill the law of Christ. (Galatians 6:2) Jesus is the unmistakable expression of the love of God, His Father. Looking at Christ and the life He led should never let us feel sorry for ourselves or unloved. For God is love. He is that love available to all, through the presence of who He is, through Him, we can be what we were meant to be.

For we are told, "He has come that we might have life, and that we might have it more abundantly." (John 10:10[b])

We must always remain available to this life we are now called to lead, and become available to the Holy Spirit who is the one to take us into such a life we are to now lead. We do not do this on our own, we must totally depend upon His presence within us to bring us there.

Now to be Christ centered, not self centered! To rid ourselves of being anything we are not called to be. To crucify it as we are told, to the cemetery church! To get our eyes off of ourselves and unto Jesus, it is this love alone that has the power to take us where God wants us to be.

The stage is being set church! The curtain is about to be pulled back! Are we in our places? Are we made into thee image of? Are we ready for all eyes to be upon us as He brings us through to that place of "Awe"?

It will be to those with a heart for God, to set their heart as His. It won't be a denomination, it won't be in a set location, it is not going to be found in a place. It will come from us, not as expected, but from the heart of the church, from within us. So we must not think because we go to that building on a Sunday makes us anymore a Christian, than for someone we don't see there every Sunday makes them not a Christian. It matters not where you attend, or even if you attend, it is a matter of the heart. Not where we go, who we know or what we are outside of Him, it is in Him that we will attain it. Not because we go to church, but because we are the church!

Being a partaker of Christ's life makes the difference. Again it is in His life coming through us to others, nothing in ourselves.

Not the act of being seen, but for Him to be seen. In life, not in a building! Yes His word says to not forsake the gathering of the brethren, we need to unite, be together as one. Yet! We must not judge because we do not see someone every Sunday, this does not mean they are not a part of us. We must submit only to love and remain in love to all.

For looks are deceiving one may even work in the highest degree of the so called "church", as contained within four walls. To look the part, talk the part, knowing scripture. Guess what?

Even satan knows the word! Don't be fooled! One might teach Sunday school, clean the office, or maybe run it! Remember he is a great deceiver, a counterfeit, be careful.

Yet all to no avail, all empty works, unless God's love is in them to now control there life. Ruling in thought and deed. Our love is manifested through our relationship with others, we can measure if we are a reflection of Christ or not. We only deceive ourselves if we do good on a Sunday for all eyes to be on us, yet our life outside of those four walls helps no one. So selfish to continue to have the appearance of, eyes only set upon yourself. It is worthless, and all of no use all these years, you have been serving a dead god, the god of religion!

"Do nothing from selfishness or deceit, but with humility of mind let each of us regard one another as more important than them self." (Philippians 2:3) We are servants of the most High God!

(Philippians 1:21) "For me to live is Christ, and to die is gain." This is our service to our God to live as Christ and in this life is our death which is gain.

Again He gave for us, Christ died so that His life might live in us!

"People will be lovers of pleasure rather than lovers of God, having a form of godliness but denying its power". (2nd Timothy 3:5)

The scripture clearly states that they will be going to Church, they will be doing things among us, they will have the "appearance of, a form of godliness." Yet at the same time, deny God's power to rule their lives.

And all of us must clothe ourselves with humility in our dealings with one another, for "God opposes the proud, but gives grace to the humble". Humble yourselves therefore under the mighty hand of God, so that He may exalt you in due time. Cast all your anxiety on Him, because He cares for you. Discipline yourselves, keep alert. Like a roaring lion your adversary the devil prowls around, looking for someone to devour. Resist him, steadfast in your faith, for you know that your brothers and sisters in all the world are undergoing the same kinds of sufferings. And after you have suffered for a little while, the God of all grace, who called you to eternal glory in Christ, will himself restore, support, strengthen, and establish you. To Him be the power forever and ever, Amen. (1st Peter 5:5-11)

It is not our position nor our status that gets us anywhere it is the hand of God, for he apposes the proud, but gives grace to the humble. So don't get proud of yourself because of where you are in the so called church. Rather you have your name on a piece of paper saying you are a member. That piece of paper will get us no where, least of all into heaven. It is God who places, who he wants, where he wants, when he wants, it is not up to us, or a so called board. Some may say if you don't have that piece of paper, you might stay the hand of God. Yet God says with it you just might stay his hand. For it is He that moves us into position, not man, nor a piece of paper. Who are we really putting our trust in? God or Man? People He is God, he can do anything he wants. Again who are we? He does not need to explain Himself to us! He will always use the foolish to confound the wise!

For I know my call is of God. I will not sooth my flesh nor not do what God asks of me, nor desires. It matters not what my flesh says nor what man says. I must only obey God and His word. It is a simple minded man that thinks this life here, or anyone here is worth anything outside of God. We must only laugh at it all as it begins to crumble beneath our feet, for one day it will be no longer. Don't be fooled into thinking differently, it and everything with it will be gone.

"Since all these things are to be dissolved in this way, what sort of persons ought you to be in leading lives of holiness and godliness, waiting for the hastening, the coming of the day of God, because of which the heavens will be set ablaze and be dissolved, and the elements will melt with fire? But, in accordance with his promise, we wait for new heavens and a new earth, where righteousness is at home". (2nd Peter 3:11-13)

Do not fool yourself into thinking any differently, it and everything with it, what has it all been worth? All our plans, our life without God. Our dreams! Of what? For what? It is all empty without Him, all your relationships with those that are not going to be with you on your death bed. It will be His face you are going to be staring into! It is your relationship with "Him", that is all that's going to matter, now and then. Pure and simple! That is it! Period!

Oh! You might say that you know Him. Oh! But I say do you know Him! "One thee knowledge of! Thee other a relationship with!" Which is it?

The word again reminds us in, (Ecclesiastes 2:1-11), as Soloman writing about his own life, discovered his wealth, power, position, women, accomplishments all held nothing for him, nor did any of it make him happy. He had it all, then in verse (11), he states, "Then I considered all that my hands had done and the toil I had spent in doing it, and again, all was vanity and a chasing after the wind, and there was nothing gained under the sun."

Here was the richest man ever, God had supplied him with everything, wealth beyond belief. Soloman learned in the end the only thing worth anything was his relationship with God. It was the only thing that truly made him happy, fulfilled, content, at peace. True happiness only comes from knowing and pleasing God, you can search the world over, look to the opposite sex for it, traveling to far off countries, money, whatever! All vanity! As Soloman tells us "like chasing the wind". And who has ever chased the wind? Let alone caught it! Our very security and self-worth are not found in things. But in the love of God!

Don't be deceived! God gave us these people in scripture as examples to learn from. But I don't know, it looks like a lot of people are out there chasing that ole wind! While you are out there running after it, satan is laughing the entire time. He will take you down the same road as many before you. Just step in! It's yours! Yours and a empty lonely life along with it, let us learn from Soloman. You will forever be chasing something to fill up that void in your life, and all along it is "He", that will fill it. (Then as now this life holds deception for us.)

The enemy is out to devour you, consume you, and make you believe a lie. As he comes and tries to deceive us, as scripture says. Satan goes about (as or like), a roaring lion. Again I looked it up! Remember the Holy Spirit is our Teacher! He is forever leading us into truth, He does not want us to be left without knowing. For he tells us "that His people will parish without knowledge".

Looking those words up, brought light to that verse for me, and set me free years ago! It shows us that satan is a great pretender! And yes he can cause harm, hurt us, and no his teeth are not pulled out! For if you've ever had him get ahold of your backside, you'd know he had teeth!

But "as", and "like", state (to resemble, or similar to, the characteristics of, in the role of, to act as, or in the way it would be). Hello! It is all a big bluff!

"Jesus"
"God's Sword"

He is a great deceiver, a pretender, a look alike, a wanna be. Satan is not like Christ! He is not the lion of Judah, nor king of anything, quit listening to him church! He is a defeated foe. He tries to bluff his way back on a ground, a position taken from him, he is a talker, don't let him wear you down.

He's bluffing you! Do you know what "Bluff", means? To fool or frighten, usually by acting in a bold or confident manner. He knows he is defeated! We must too! We must quit giving ground to a defeated foe, and stand!

He's bluffing! Just like my husband did to me for years, and held me captive in fear of what he might do to me. Satan does the same thing, where do you think these people get it from! He does the same thing to the body of Christ, and he has been able to get away with it!

You might not have an abusive husband, but you have been held captive. If not the body of Christ wouldn't be in the shape it's in! Church, pull his bluff! Leave his ways, his lies, do not listen to him anymore, walk out! You will loosen his hold he has over you and his power over you will come to a halt. Submit to God, resist the devil, and he will flee from you! You are victorious church! It is time we stood up and acted like it, and take back what is ours. Saying enough is enough! No more!

In fact, there are many of you that as you read that part of my life with my husband, probably said to yourself some things like this. What is wrong with her? Why didn't she get out? Why did she stay with him? She must have liked it, other wise she would have left! Or she probably deserved it! I have heard it all.

Now I ask you that same thing! Do you like it? Why do you stay? What is wrong with you? Why do you put up with him? Get out! Why church do we stay in his clutches? Day in and day out, listening to all the lies and putting up with his abuse. Pretending all is well, and you are tucked in your safe little life of no need! Afraid to do anything for fear of what he might do to you. Church it is time to get away from your "spiritual abuser," satan, and pull his bluff!

Or maybe you're the abuser within the church! You have only been kidding yourself if you think you are safe. It is all a huge worthless game on your part, God sees it all. Or haven't you read the word lately? Or maybe you have and you are above it, and it doesn't apply to you. That's right only the ones lower than you are subject to it, right? Your mask is about to be pulled! For God is rising up a people within a people, within the church that are going to stand up as Christ did. And say no more! And begin to turn the tables over!

The pretence, the control, the anger, the manipulation, the sarcasm, all about to stop and be called out! The abuse within the Body, the Church! All coming to a halt, or have we forgot who lives in us? You and me, the Body of Christ, now house Him. Every finger, word, thought, or deed done to another brother or sister, a believer, one of God's children. He has seen and heard it all! Do you really think you would get away with it? Maybe all those years around the people that thought as you did, maybe cause they stuck with you. Instead of sticking to God, and His ways. Our very Creator has been subject to it all, He is so grieved. But there is a people that God is now rising up to stand against this, for nothing has been hid! Have we forgotten "He", is all seeing, all knowing!

Let us go to (2 Kings 2:23-25), and see what happened when men made fun of and touched one of God's messengers and paid for it with their lives.

"As Elisha was going on his way, some young men came out of the city and jeered at him, saying, "Go away bald head"! When he turned around and saw them, he cursed them in the name of the Lord. Then two she-bears came out of the woods and mauled forty-two of them.

These men did not like that he went about and talked of their immorality as Elijah had done before him. They were not merely teasing him, but they were showing severe disrespect for a messenger of God's and God's power. God sent the judgement for their callous behavior.

Let us go now to (Psalm 105:12-15), when they were few in number, of little account, and strangers in it, wandering from nation to nation, from kingdom to another people, he "God", allowed no one to oppress them; he rebuked kings on their account, saying, "Do not touch my anointed ones; do my prophets no harm."

"God the same yesterday, today, and forever." (Hebrews 13:8) He has not changed, He is faithful to His word in more ways than one.

Church! We need to stop while we still have time, we are only spiritually wounding and killing each other off, some are even left for dead. It is sad to agree that "Christians are the only ones that wound their own and leave them to die on the battlefield". What is wrong with us? Do we not know that these ways are not from God? We should not have "friendly fire" amongst the brethren.

My foster daughter that was killed came to my mind a while back, I thought that is odd, where did that come from Lord? He spoke! It is the shape of my church! No Lord, I replied! How? Show me!

He did! There are murderers who in secret think no one sees them or is looking, as they go about killing my children with rejection, slicing them up with their tongues, words of judgement! Dismembering them with isolation and then to have their hearts contained in concrete, leaving them hard towards me! They do not care, they continue on, the body parts then scattered throughout the land left to think no one knows they are out there! Maybe buried in silence, some think! Some baby's within the church, like my baby that watched it all, affected for life. Others as the wife, left in the cold to what is even happening around them!

These only lead a carnal life led by death! They must only now question who they serve! I cried as God gave me this parable, "an earthly story, with a heavenly message."

Church do we leave the ninety-nine safe sheep within the fold to go look where the one has gone that is missing? Or do we really care? Do we know why they have gone astray? Are they wounded? Left out there for the wolves to devour? Are they hurt? Are they crying out for us to come help them fit back in the fold? There again safe under the protection of the older sheep, under the shepard! Do we honestly care what is happening around us? Are we seeking after the heart of God as David? Are we? Are we really so deceived, or just selfish?

Where is our compassion? Our mercy? Our love? Where are we? Who are we? What church have we become?

We need to know that God's heart is broken! Does this even bother us? Do we not even care for Him? Are we so self centered, so consumed with ourselves, us a supposedly dead person? And yet we stand in judgement of what the Jews did to Him! Are we so different? Are we really? Has man's heart been torn as His, has our heart been broken? Do we have it too good? What has happened to us? We are no different than the world, yet He tells us to come out from among them and be separate. Yet it seems as if we have come to place of merely just fitting in with them, the world! This is not what he died for! Do we too not call for BARABAS?

We need to repent church! Turn and never go back to such ways. For nothing is worth being separated from God, we should never want to stay in a place of such grossness.

Repent means for us to feel more than sorry, it requires to feel sorrowful, remorse about something we have done that is wrong. To change one's mind, regret it, never to do it again. This is how you can tell if one has truly repented or they are merely sorry, repentance requires action on our part, sorry does not!

He knows our hearts, He sees rather we are meaning it or not! We cannot fool Him! He sees it all! Go after His heart church, see these things as does He.

This is why God has not come upon us the church in the fullness of who He is or in the power of what He can do. His word plainly tells us to not grieve the Holy Spirit!

"And do not grieve the Holy Spirit of God, which you were sealed with for the day of redemption. Let "all bitterness", and "wrath" and "anger" and "clamor", and "slander" be out away from you, along with all "malice".

And be kind to one another, "tenderhearted", "forgiving" each other, just as "God in Christ has forgiven you"! Therefore be imitators of God, as beloved children; "walk in love", just as Christ also loved you, and "gave Himself up for us", an offering and a sacrifice to God as a fragrant aroma. (Ephesians 4:30-5:2)

As "God in Christ has forgiven us"! What a beautiful verse church! And again who are we? Are we even above this, when God isn't! He forgave us even "in" Christ and what He did for us, upon his death on the cross! Oh God!

And we church are asked here to do the same thing, and by the holy presence of God residing within us we too can do this. Our lifestyles hurt Him, our attitudes towards each other is harmful to the body as well. Not forgiving and to hold a grudge is placing ourselves even above God! For He does not even stay in such a place. Why then should we church stay there? We cause Him sorrow by doing these things mentioned in the above verse of scripture.

With my husband, and some of the other things in my life. I know the enemy tried his hardest to hold me in a place of unforgiveness, then the Lord came and lovingly had me take this scripture to heart. I saw that if I chose to remain in a place of unforgiveness I was putting myself above God! A place where satan wants us all. Why? For here he knows he's got us! This is the position that satan took when he was cast down, to eternally be separated from God. He (satan) had placed himself above God!

We too do this very same thing by listening to him, instead of to God our Father. We need to be careful, this is how good deception can get, one does not even know it's happening. And then, one day! We are caught in the snare!

We must only do as our heavenly Father tells, to love as He. For remember love covers a multitude of sins! This is why we have to stay obedient to the call of love on our lives. To do as the Father asks of us, for He really does know what is best for us.

We must not fool ourselves into thinking that "He", will come to us and pour Himself out upon all this. If we continue and not go before the feet of our Lord Jesus, to be broken of self. Or remain intact as is, vessels of only looks, but of no use. What are we here for? As our example before us so gave, so must we now give, of ourselves to remain no longer the same.

"For the multitude of those who believed were of "one heart", and of "one soul", this we are told in (Acts 4:32) Jesus says to us for if a kingdom is divided against itself it will not stand! (Mark 3:24) We know that satan comes to divide, it is he who brings division, and now you know why. He keeps us down, so we won't be able to stand!" He (satan) has brought this division between us!

(Acts 2:1) We are told they were, "all together in one place", this is where the power is, in one accord! They were united spiritually as one!

The Spirit is searching hearts today, to see who has this oneness of heart, to be united as one, to be able to stand as one!

Church do we see why we have no power? Again lets go back to where God began with me, to our original scripture in (Luke 7:37-50). The vessel must be broken open, before it's true worth within can then be poured out. You can not get something out of it if it remains unable to be opened up. Like us! We need to be honest with ourselves and open up before God, not hold back, giving all we hold inside, up to Him!

We prove our love for Him by our obedience towards Him. If we love Him we will obey Him. Amen! If we only look the part, it is all of no worth, we have only been spinning our wheels. We church can tithe, go to church, dress the part, sing all the songs, work in all the right ministries. These are all "FLESH", if we are not totally surrendered to the hand of God. If we do not have love, all is a waste of time on our part. All wasted if we are not being shaped into the "Image of a vessel of use". He is the potter, we are the clay! Molded and fashioned into the image of Christ! This alone is our goal!

See the enemy has been able to keep us handicapped all these years, unable to move properly because of these things. Many things paralyze us from within, anger, fear, unforgiveness, pride, jealousy, control, judgement, religion, just plain oh self! Keeping us locked up in a spiritual wheelchair. Why do we remain to be handicapped church? Do we like to be able not to move freely?

We are even handicapped to believe a lie, and not the truth! Even though the enemy is defeated as God's word tells us, we still believe him! Why? Even though the enemy comes to rob, kill and destroy us, doesn't mean we need to let him. If you had a robber, a killer in your neighborhood, and it is posted to be aware! Would you be opening your door up to anyone just a knockin? No way! You'd be prepared to blow him away! No difference spiritually! He's out there, just quit opening up the door! Submit to God, resist the devil and he will flee from you.

Your security sign is posted out front to detour him, it's the blood of Jesus. Let your enemy get close, just whip out your sword, and he is a goner. He is not going to take on a child of God, literally to come at you. That is why he must deceive, like he did in the garden. He questioned God's authority, and Eve fell for it. Have we not learned anything?

Acting as, resembling, like a roaring lion, or as a known counterfeit of Christ's attributes. Satan is limited by God! Satan only deceives and imitates, he is a defeated foe remember that! Defeated by the blood of the Lamb and the word of our testimony. He will try and divert us, from our mission in life just as he did to Christ before us. For when Jesus walked this earth he walked as us, as a man. Tempted as we are, yet He stood his ground.

Jesus stood upon the word of His Father, this kept satan from destroying His mission in life, the call He was so purposed for. Satan misinterprets the scriptures, tries to control us, instills fear in many a saints. It should not be this way church! Do we really understand our place "in" Christ Jesus?

Read in (Isaiah 14:12-18), especially verses 16 and 18, "Those who will stare at you, and ponder over you; "IS THIS THE MAN WHO MADE THE EARTH TREMBLE, WHO WOULD NOT LET HIS PRISONERS GO HOME"? This is him?

When God showed me this, I thought this reminds me of the old feeble man behind the smoke screen in the Wizard of Oz! He fooled everyone! Until one day his façade was found out and made clear to all! It was all done in deceit! He was never questioned! They too bought into a lie! See satan will take all that “we give him”! You know a smoke screen is a dense cloud of smoke used to keep the enemy from seeing movements of troops. Not no more!

Satan does not want you or I to go home to be with our Father, so he will do all he can to keep us from Him. To keep us prisoners all locked up in ourselves. We must remember that Jesus has the key to our freedom! We are not held captive we are free! And whom the Son sets free is free indeed!

See pride was satan’s sin, which is against God and resulted in his ultimate judgement. We church are vulnerable to make the very same mistake. Do not ever be too proud to call upon the name of Jesus, God’s Son who died for us, so that we wouldn’t be held captive in a lie. So that we might not be held in deceit by satan and to eternally live with him, separated from our Father.

Let us not listen to him any more church! Let us only now go to His extended hand of love, allowing Him to gently break us of what is not of Him, and bring us to a point of use in Him.

“For the Lord knows who are His, and let everyone who names the name of the Lord abstain from wickedness”.

Now in a large house there are not only gold and silver vessels, but also vessels of wood and of earthenware, and some to honor and some to dishonor.

Therefore, “IF”, a man cleanses himself from these things, he will be a vessel of honor, sanctified, useful to the Master, prepared for every good work.

Now flee from youthful lust, and pursue righteousness, faith, love, and peace, with those who call on the Lord from a pure heart. (2nd Timothy 2:19-22)

The scripture that heads this is, “The firm foundation of God stands, having a seal!” This seal is the Holy Spirit, He is God’s seal to us, yet He tells us here “Let everyone who names the name of the Lord abstain, or refrain from wickedness.” Refrain means to keep one self back by choice! God leaves this choice to us church, He waits for us to come to a place of surrender on our own. The Holy Spirit will come along side of us as our helper, our comforter, our teacher, to direct us back to the Father, never away from. Remember that is what Jesus did also, He always directed, pointed back to the Father, He kept nothing for Himself. We are being continually led to the Father, He also draws us to Himself.

I also looked up "seal", it is an instrument for pressing, stamping, putting an official mark into something, as to indicate official status, quality; also it keeps something firmly closed; something that confirms or makes certain. That was so sweet to me when I read it, He does it all for us, God gave again of Himself to us, we are in that firm foundation (Jesus), and we are meant to stand! See that too for a divine purpose, for even when satan sees us, he sees us in that place where God put us, in Christ Jesus.

That is why it is so important to remain "in" Him, to do all and then to stand. It is in that position, that stand, that satan remains defeated, for when we stand in Him, we are hid! Satan only sees Jesus, not us! That is why he has to come and fool, deceive, lie, to get us away from that stand. He knows he can't touch us when we are submitted to God, he can't get passed the blood nor the seal!

"Jesus"
"God's Life"

Enough is enough! We have no reason to stay down, we are not the defeated ones, nor are we licked. The enemy has roared for way too long church, and detoured us off track. We are not each others enemy, we do not fight against one another, we have but "one enemy". God tell us this is His word, our enemy is satan, not you or I, but him!

Time to start turning those tables over church as did our example Christ, before us, and all for the same reasons that we remain to have today.

Only two truths remain aside from God's word! That is that He is right and that we are wrong!

"But we have this treasure in clay jars, so that it may be made clear that this extraordinary power belongs to God and does not come from us. We are afflicted in every way, but not crushed; perplexed, but not driven to despair; persecuted, but not forsaken; struck down but not destroyed; always carrying in the body the death of Jesus, so that the life of Jesus may be made visible in our bodies.

For while we live, we are always being given up to death for Jesus' sake, so that the life of Jesus may be made visible in our mortal flesh!" (2 Cor. 4:7-12)

Here too we are reminded that we are these clay jars that contains this powerful presence of God, the Holy Spirit, we are His dwelling place. And it shows us also that no matter what it is that we go through, it is this inner strength of the power of God that lives in us that will bring us through.

For while we live, we are always being given up to death for Jesus' sake, so that the life of Jesus may be made visible in our flesh, through our death, so that He may live and not us.

Remembering we are clay, yet containers at the same time, vessels of His use to do as He Wills. For remember we are dead! How can we now still live and want our own way? Does a dead man raise from the grave to say what he wants? Or even that he doesn't want to be dead? Did he have a choice in the matter? Do we? If we are really God's, this must and will be made known. For we will be known by our fruit that we bear here on this earth. They will know we are Christians by our love!

He promises to be with us through our trials, our hardships, our sufferings, not to spare us from them. Our faith to be tested with each step of life, our faith in Christ is to bring blessings, yet at the same time great sufferings too.

For God calls us to commitment not to comfort! You think Jesus was comfortable in what He had to do, you think He had to not suffer? And we want to partake of His life, His blessings, His glory, and to stay clear from such as what He went through.

If so, then you had better get out now! For to be a partaker of Christ is to partake of his death also, we are called to lay it all down at His feet.

For if you find yourself in a place of comfort, your easy chair positioned back, your feet up, remote in hand, you see all as well around you! Guess what? The enemy has you exactly where he wants you, comfortable, complacent, and off guard!

If you are a people pleaser, if it means something to you to be liked by others! Guess what? The enemy has you too right where he wants you! Your eyes on your self, for you aren't about to die to any one not liking you!

We must choose to obey God, rather than to seek comfort or the approval of those around us. Or do you feel it is to benefit you?

To be in the "in crowd", only leaves you out of God's crowd! His people don't move in those kinds of circles, to be popular or liked is of no use to those truly focused on "Him".

Or maybe you sing in the choir, or teach Sunday school? Oh, you do all the right things before man. Yet when every one's back is turned you snub a brother or sister down town! Watch out! The enemy has you too right where he wants you too! Safe in the arms of deceit! You had better run from his arms fast, for soon they will crush you. Instead of you crushing him under your feet!

We had better start proving just who we serve! It isn't worth all that anyway! What has anyone really done to you for you to treat them like that? What is the big deal? Oh! That's right! They are beneath you! Yet I thought I read in God's word we are one body! Members one of thee other! Then if God's word doesn't tell us to act like this to each other! I wonder who does? Do you need a hint?

Oh no, you don't physically strike someone or yell at them, or to curse. You don't have to! Your heart has spoken for you! It is clear to them and to God where you stand.

Or maybe all your invitations are out, and that one person you just so happened to over look, wasn't included! You really don't care either that is part of the pain you like to inflict as you play your petty game! Watch out! The enemy has you too, right where he wants you! They too know as well as God the game you play, and it is funny how we say we serve God, go to church, give money, etc. Yet none of these things are from him, he tells us none of this, we do it all on our own.

Have we no fear? Do we not know who we serve? He has seen and heard it all! Here too you have been only kidding yourself, you have deceived yourself too. You pose no threat to satan, he laughs at you as you alone weave your web of deceit, as you are about to be entangled in it yourself. It will be your down fall, and he sits back and laughs at it all, again he doesn't have to do a thing. We do it for him! It's a sad day church!

Are you still wondering why God hasn't come to us, in all that He is? Would you?

God says in (Proverbs 6:16), "there are six things He hates seven that are an abomination to Him: haughty eyes, a lying tongue, and hands that shed innocent blood, a heart that devises wicked plans, feet that hurry to run to evil, a lying witness who testifies falsely, and one who sows discord among brethren!

Ouch! We sure don't see anything visible here do we that would cause harm, that is because it is all done in deceit! And if you are one that gives ear to such a person, you too had better run as far away as you can from them. Stop listening to them!

For God won't stand for much more of this childish behavior! For once we were children and acted as such! But we are mature now and have left this kind of behavior behind us! Or have we? Is the bottle still hanging out of our mouths church? Especially if you are up in years of being a Christian, and you are remaining to play these games. It's time you stepped up to the burial plot and jumped in, you are running short of time. You better not only get your shovel, you had better get a taste of what it's like to be separated from God. For you think you are safe? Guess again! He's letting you know who you have made your God! Yourself!

"But when the complete comes, the partial will come to an end. When I was a child; I spoke like a child, thought like a child, I reasoned like a child; when I became an adult, I put away childish ways." (1 Corinthians 13:10)

All a bad taste in God's mouth, detestable, loathing, a thing we should all stay clear of. Plus what has it all been for? A waste of time! Of no use! For when we stand before God, how are we to answer for such behavior?

Believe me, whatever your answer is, it is not going to be of any worth to the Lord on that day. Nothing we could say is about to make Him change His mind, and still not then find it all "abominable". He isn't going to change for us!

God doesn't care what position we hold in between those four walls where we attend on a Sunday. If we are not truly serving, loving the body of Christ on a daily basis outside those walls, when every one's eyes are on us. On that one day of the week, we have only been working our flesh! Or do we have selective service in those that we care to help! Those that only fit into our circle!

Oh, he has you now! Right where he wants us! Church, satan has been playing this game of "religion", for thousands of years. You'd think we would have learned by now! No wonder we are called sheep!

None of our so called self-righteous deeds amount to a thing, nor do they stand for anything. Here again flesh on our part, carnal deeds of someone that remains to be alive to their old man, instead of alive in Christ!

All done in vain and worthless all those years behind us wasted and of no use. Or even if you've stood before people on a Sunday and received recognition for anything. You have received your reward! That of man!

"For if you speak in tongues of angels, but do not have love you are a noisy gong or a clanging cymbal. And if you have prophetic powers, and understand all mysteries and all knowledge, and if you have all faith, so as to remove mountains, but do not have love, "you are nothing". If you give all your possessions, and if you hand your body over so that you may boast, but do not have love, "you gain nothing!"

For love is patient; love is kind; love is not envious or boastful or arrogant or rude. It does not insist on it's own way; it is not irritable or resentful; it does not rejoice in wrongdoing but rejoices in the truth. It bears all things, believes all things, endures all things, Love never ends. (1 Cor. 13:1-8)

Again we can put ourselves in check by God's word, either we are, or we are not! We can only do it through the Holy Spirit that lives in us, we must give up to remaining to self, give up to the stronger one that lives within.

"The sacrifice acceptable to God is a broken spirit; a broken and contrite heart, O God, you will not despise." (Psalm 51:17)

We can never please God by our outward actions, no matter how good they may seem to us or look to others. It is only our "inner heart attitude", that amounts to anything of worth to our Lord!

He wants our hearts, as a man described by God Himself, David was a man after God's own heart. (1st Samuel 13:14) A man after His own heart, that is important, his confessions were from the heart. And his repentance was also genuine, David as a man was a man of great wrong doing before God. He never took lightly his loving relationship with God, he always came before Him and repented. God saw his heart and was honored by his love for Him. He not only knew God, but he knew Him in a intimate way, as always wanting to be close, and have nothing come between them.

God the same yesterday, today and forever. (Hebrews 13:8) He wants the same from us today, no difference. He is the same, without change!

We are the same as David, we too have a chance to be after God's heart! This is why we shouldn't be tearing at each other, gossiping, back biting, to carry tales, or to listen to them. We were meant to build each other up, serve, strengthen the body, and to love one another. Not to tear it apart! Don't forget the least we do unto one of these we have done it unto Him!

Do we understand this concept? We are one body? All having different parts to do, many members, yet one functioning body. Us the church! "ONE".

Then why are we committing spiritual suicide? The way we keep at each other cutting each other up! Maybe a leg, a arm, a toe, pulling at the bowels, stomach or a lung. We need all of these parts of the body, rather physically or spiritually, to function the way it was intended to do. You would never slug yourself in the stomach or cut your lung from your body, ripping off your ear, or to cut off a toe. Would you?

Then why would we do this spiritually to the "Body of Christ?" This is why we don't function as we are supposed to. "Function", means to have the proper action, use or purpose, to operate or work properly, a quantity whose "value depends on the value of another quantity". Get the picture?

We should be so ashamed of what we have done to God's heart, have we not learned anything? Church it is better that we take care of all this here, while we have the time. And the hand of grace is upon us! I do not think this is anything to be proud of or something we'd be wanting to take home with us, before the Father.

I would much rather be humbled and broken here, than there! Church He is extending His hand of Grace to us, we need to take hold of it while we still can.

His grace is with us now, but not for long church! We have been spoiled little children, wanting our own way. We'll get it alright and everything else that comes along with it. Nothing!

Stay as we are and believe God has no concern over all of this, and what's been going on! He is a push over right? He won't do anything, surely will He? You had better read the "Word of God", God is the same yesterday, today, and forever. Remember?

Lets look at the story of "Noah", God spoke, and who listened? Who was let in? What about "Sodom and Gamorrah," what was told to them, how many got out? Who was spared in both cases? Or maybe the "Promised Land", is a better example for us! How many were left out? And why?

We better believe what God says, and know He means what He says and says what He means. Don't kid yourself! He wasn't messing around then, and He's not messing around now!

Church we are never going to come this way again, we pass through but once, we are not reincarnated to live it over. This here and now is our chance, we get but one shot at this. What's it gonna be? It is time we focus on Him and get our eyes off ourselves and each other, and get on with it!

He is a God of honor, love, truth and respect and will settle for nothing less than our obedience and love towards Him.

Just as with Abraham, and his son Isaac. God did not want Abraham's son as a sacrifice! God wanted Abraham's "obedience". He was asked to go! He did! And God honored that. Abraham's faith is an example of which we are a seed to, is it growing?

The story of what happened when God asked Abraham is in (Genesis 22:1-19), and his faith in God was spoken in verse (5). Abraham states, "Stay here with the donkey; the boy and I will go over there; we will worship, and (we will come back to you).

This is the kind of faith we are called to church! He did not look at his circumstances, Abraham kept his eyes on God, and what He had promised him. God said it, Abraham knew God did not lie, therefore he knew God would not allow harm to come to his son. Yet, Abraham was being tested by God! As we are! The purpose? To strengthen our character and to deepen our commitment to Him. Abraham obeyed God, and God honored that, Abraham learned to trust God no matter what it looked like, or felt like.

Knowing God would provide, as should we! See God is always faithful! It's us that leaves Him! Abraham was being tested, as now is our faith!

Obedience is better than sacrifice! And if you love me (God), you will obey me! You will keep my commandments. See we demonstrate our love for God by our obedience towards Him. He is not looking at what you do in a building once a week on a Sunday! He is looking at what you do daily towards the body that now contains His presence here on earth.

So how are we doing? Are we doing good? As did Christ towards others? Or are we doing good! As in our state of how we feel? Self has entered in and taken place of where only Christ should be. We need to move over, get out of the way, and cease to want to have our own way! Self even say's some things like this; oh I'll never make it! I just don't fit in! It's too hard! I'm not good enough! They will never understand! I'm too tired! I just can't stop!

These are all flesh too! These are feelings! These are dangerous! These are all self talking! To feel sorry for our self has no place in God's kingdom!

This is not the example Christ set for us, for it is dangerous ground to be on. Remember feelings and sight will drown us in the misery of self, and then what? No one is coming to our party but us, we will only grow old and be alone as we entertain this flesh of ours. God came to deliver us from our "SELF".

For the sacrifice acceptable to God is a "broken spirit", as we are told in (Psalm 51:16-17). This shows it is in nothing we do! It is in what we are! "Broken"! Are we ready yet to sit at His feet? So He can begin to break us of all that is not of Him, so that He can reveal the true worth within us?

Have you been wounded? Let down? Abandoned by family? Betrayed by friends? Left out? Isolated? Good! God has you right where He needs you, and can use you. Wholly depended upon Him for your needs! For God is a jealous God, and does not intend on us going anywhere but to Him for our needs. He isn't about to share us with anyone or anything! Nor will He!

“Jesus”
“God’s Will”

Philippians 3:7-11, explains how we have Him for our all in all, “What once was gain to us, we now count these a loss for Christ, for the excellence of the knowledge of Christ Jesus my Lord, for whom I have suffered the loss of all things and count them as rubbish, that I may “gain Christ”, and be “found in Him”, not having my own righteousness, which is from the law, but which is through faith in Christ, the righteousness which is “from God by faith”; that I may “know Him” and the “power of His resurrection”, and the “fellowship of His sufferings”, being conformed to His death! In order that I may attain to the resurrection from the dead! And the fellowship of His sufferings!” Are we there Church?

See church, we have been just but dipping our toes into the water, we must go deeper into Him! You remember the scripture of when the men were fishing, and Jesus said launch out into deep waters! We must now begin to cast our nets out into that deep water enabling us to catch with love as did He. In Luke 5:4, “Jesus states this, to launch out into deep waters and let down your nets for a catch” this is also spiritually church! Look at the word, see how He speaks, it is in parables and also in many ways flip flopped. He does this now as then. And Simon Peter answered Jesus saying, “Master, we have toiled all night and caught nothing; nevertheless at (your word I will), let down the net”. He obeyed the Lord in what He said to him, and the results were over flowing. We have yet to cast out into those deep waters church!

We are to be fishers of men, not to bask in an aquarium! Leading all to love by love. To the Father, into the life of Christ, lead by the indwelling Holy Spirit! We have much to do church, we must no longer toil all night and catch nothing spiritually. We must come into the light and cast our nets now deep, no longer to only wade in shallow water.

We will get there if we die to ourselves and do as He asks, as did Simon Peter, when he said at “YOUR WILL”, Master, “I

WILL". It is by faith of what was told to him by the Lord that produced this catch that gave them even more faith.

They couldn't see it in the natural, yet when Jesus spoke, they trusted him and obeyed. The Lord brought the increase, not them, when they saw what He had done spiritually they had their faith built up. Then they knew it was in Him! They too moved and had this increase, by casting out and in faith believing.

Then they forsook all and followed Him, as we must now also do. Forsaking all for the call He is leading us into, to not remain at the surface treading water any longer. But now to dive in and go for the "pearl of great price".

Remember in (2nd Timothy 2:19-22), when he spoke of the large house that there are many vessels, different uses. But the vessel which cleanses himself from these things, he will be a vessel of honor, useful to the Master, prepared for every good work.

Well we church are this house, we the many vessels, He is the Master of this house. We are His house, bought and paid for, nothing is owed, it is paid in full, the down payment, the blood of Jesus. No note is held, the blood contains this cleansing power that we so need to become useful. And it gives life to all who remain at His feet, with a submitting heart, broken and contrite. Broken here means to be humbled church, of which I think we all need a little of! Contrite here means to be deeply and humbly sorrowful for having done wrong.

By doing this we are allowed to go deeper into Him, to reach for that pearl, He only awaits us to come to Him. To that love that He is, that no one, or no thing can bring us to, but Him!

We know what to do church! To unite in love, in Him! Standing in what Christ did for us, no longer to stumble around in the darkness, but to be brought into the light, into Jesus, of which is that light. He is the light of the world, and now we stand in His stead, so now we shine forth this light. We should not continue to hide our light under a basket of fears, lies, burdens, He has come to set the captive free. And whom the Son sets free is free indeed! He is our freedom from bondages that hold us so tight to ourselves. We need to reach out, spread forth our arms and loosen that hold that so tightly has kept us from going deeper into Christ. To now dive in deeper, for pearls are only found in deep waters!

The Holy Spirit is our breath of life, He will not let us drown, He is our sustainer of this life that we now must lead.

And yes we know what to do, and so does the enemy, he is watching our every move. But the restrainer, the Holy Spirit holds him back from us. The enemy has kept us at each other, he didn't need to come and literally destroy us. He did it from within our own ranks, bringing this division amongst the brethren. Then he has just sat back and watched us destroy ourselves, his weapon was a lie to use us one against the other. Rather it be with a person, or an entire denomination he infiltrated and broke rank. We have been warned, too, we knew, we just let him do this. We knew all of what was happening was not of God, yet we were so lazy, so comfortable, so complacent. In this stand we took he had us, and he knew it, all because we listened to a lie, instead of the truth.

Because of who we are in Christ Jesus, to keep us separated, we the body, so we won't join in ranks and forces to conquer. You think satan wants you or I to know who we are "in" Christ Jesus! Not on your life! He has been up to this same old trick for thousands of years, and we have played right into his hands.

But he knows his time is running out, that is why he's not holding anything back. And neither should we, he doesn't have anything anyways, we do, and he knows it.

He needs to read the back of the book and see exactly what is about to happen, for it is all about to change. For he holds nothing back now so get ready church! For soon he will halt! For now we too hold nothing back! Amen!

For God! He in all that He is, is about to come onto the scene. Satan knows this, the angels know this, and we too had better know this. For if you don't know what is about to happen church, you'll never know, nor will you be ready.

"Jesus"
"God's Heart"

You know all we have to do is read the word to see if we have progressed any. And sad to say, we have not.

In (Genesis 6:5-6), it says, "The Lord saw that the wickedness of humankind was great in the earth, and the Lord was sorry that He made humankind on earth, and it grieved Him to His heart. Down a few verses we see, "But Noah", found favor in the sight of the Lord. Noah wholeheartedly loved God, and also obeyed Him as well.

God was not admitting He made a mistake in creating us, instead it was His sorrow expressed for what the people turned to. God was sorry that the people chose sin and death instead of a "relationship", with Him. The people's sin grieved God's heart, it remains the same today church! Again! "God the same yesterday, today, and forever". (Hebrews 13:8)

But Noah pleased God, far from perfect, yet Noah found favor in the sight of the Lord. In spite of the sin going on around him, Noah continued on to do that which God asked of him.

Are there any Noah's out there today? Do we see the heart of God, then or now church? Or are we still so occupied with ourselves, that we have forgotten the hand that fashioned us? His life that was breathed into us? We have nothing and we are nothing outside of Him! Our breath! His! Our life! His! Our will! His!

You think you've done it all these years on your own? Guess again! It is He alone that started our heart, gave us breath, brought us life! Try and do any of this on your own! You will soon find out, who and what is your source! It is only He!

We have this life within us! That will make this change of heart, it is not us, we are totally depended upon Him. It is time to submit to Him, for the good of mankind as well as for the good of the church, and most importantly for the good of God's heart!

“Little children you are from God, and have conquered them; for the one who lives in you is greater than the one who is in the world.” (John 4:4)

O God! I pray we see the truth in your word, bring your light to us. Move in and through us your church, use us to bring glory to your name. Let us only see you and not ourselves, let us obey and sit at your feet. Forgive us Father!

We have Him! His word tells us this, what are we so afraid of? We are not the one’s on the run! It is satan! We shouldn’t be afraid to stand up, to make a difference. No matter what we face in this life, or how it feels. We have already conquered him, by the blood of Jesus! The word tells us this, and the word does not and can not lie! The evil that prevails in the world around us is not stronger than God our Father. The mighty presence that lives in us, the Holy Spirit, assures us of this, as well as does God’s word, Jesus!

For the Son of God was revealed to destroy the works of the devil! Anything that satan brings our way is to detour us from our “center” of life. And that is God Himself! The center of it all within us church! Satan cannot stand this, that is why he acts as he does, he will do all he can get away with to get our attention off of God. And unto himself! The source of self himself! Satan!

This is the victory that conquers the world, our faith. Who is it that conquers the world but the one who believes that Jesus is the Son of God. (1 John 5:4-5) Church our faith is being tested!

Again God said it, not man. We must believe in His word. This remember is our sword! This kind of faith is the opposite of what we see. It is believing no matter what in the word of God. God’s word even says, that anything not of faith is a sin! To doubt God and His word, Jesus! Is a sin! You don’t have to be involved in sex outside of marriage, murder, lying, or not forgive. Just not believe! Doubt God!

This too will separate you from His presence! Anything that is sin removes us from a relationship with Him! Doubt is sin! To not believe God is sin!

And yes our faith will be tested when we face trials, it shows our trust in God. “For whenever we face trials of any kind consider it nothing but joy, because you know the testing of your faith produces endurance; and let endurance have its full effect, so that you may be "mature", and "complete", lacking in nothing." (James 1:2-4) in vs. 3.

Our very character is being molded through our trials, they are only opportunities for our growth. This scripture tells us when we face trials, not if. If you're a Christian, you had better see some trials, otherwise you are not growing or being tested. Careful! They are beneficial to our growth into the image of Jesus. If He was tested, we will be tested.

The results to be manifested in our hearts, to change them, break them, and mold them, not to remain the same old man. Keeping us distant from our Creator, but, to draw us to Him. "Draw near to God and He will draw near to you." This is in (James 4:8), He waits to see our heart towards Him, we are asked to draw near to Him, and He will draw near to us.

When all is said and done, if we obey, we will be broken and useable by our "Maker". To be broken of self, to continue to sit at the feet of Jesus, allowing the gentle hand of our Lord to come and cleanse us of all that is not of Him. To reveal "the image of", His very Son, Christ. For the same that He did, we will do, and more.

And then watch out! For the gates of Hell shall not prevail against us the church! Get ready to "Shake, Rattle, and Roll". Shake the foundations of Heaven with our lives, as a prayer. Rattle the gates of Hell and every Principality of darkness with the power contained within us, the Holy Spirit. And "Roll", back the stone that hold the captives, and say Lazares come forth.

These days are upon church! Are we ready? Are we willing to obey and stand up to do all the Father asks of us? We should be excited church! To be alive at a time such as this! We have been kept for this specific time. God has kept His best for last! Us! You and I! We should be jumpin' church!

Do you know this? Have you ever thought, why me? And why now? Well it is all a part of God's plan, before time, this time in our life to be now! It is a great day to be His chosen children now, see even He knows we are coming through. It too in His plans and predestined, all held till now. Just for you and me!

We have no time to keep our eyes on each other anymore, we now should be gazing into the eyes that saved us. Into the eyes of Jesus! We are not defeated church! And satan knows it! We are the calm before the Storm!

Get ready church! God has waited for us, this day, this moment in time, even before time. Our faith should be risen in great hopes of what is about to happen around us. God is ready to pour Himself out, of us, His church! Are we ready to be broken, so He can come forth, and do the Will of God?

We are the extension of Him, His love, and that love is in us. How can we not do it? Together we are a never ending circle of love. He to us, and we to Him. It cannot be broken. His word tells us nothing can separate us from the love of God. "No, in all things we are more than conquerors through Him who loved us. For I am convinced that neither death, nor life, nor angels, nor depth, nor anything else in all creation, will be able to separate us from the love of God in Christ Jesus our Lord." (Romans 8:37-39)

The devil can not stand this love! The love of the Father for us His children, nor can he stand for us to love our Father. This is why he has fought so hard to bring this division between the brethren, for it is a place he will never be able to be in. He lost all rights, his pride came between their relationship. That is why, satan likes for us to question God! To ask why! Why me Lord? For God is the source of everything we are to be, and have yet to become.

Let us give the Father what He wants church! Like us He wants to be loved! See in more ways than one, we are made in His image. He too has waited for us, as we do for Him. See the source of our love is also the object of our love!

A complete circle, it is never ending, nor can it be broken! It is complete in itself, "LOVE", of which is God!

What else is there church? We are going to spend eternity with Him as well as with each other, so we might as well get a jump start on it down here! Let us so love, for we were made from love, to love! It is all contained in the act of love! We have this love within us, this is the reason we can do it. It is "He", that will do it, not us, we must now only give in, submit, yield, surrender, lay it all down at His feet!

To be broken so that the true love that resides within each one of us can be poured out from us to a dying world. It is our choice! He will not make us do anything, it will be because we now so choose to, as did He when He gave. What are we to give? We can stay down and be defeated or rise up in who we are "in Christ Jesus", and in the power of the Holy Spirit, in us, letting God the Father have His way. Which is perfect! Amen!

"Jesus"
"God's Purpose"

For we know all things work together for good for those who love God, who are called according to "His Purpose". (Romans 8:28)

You see God is working to fulfill His purpose, not to make us happy! Through our trials, in them all we gain a wealth of treasure not of this earth, for me this world holds nothing I want. I like Soloman have learned it is as to chase the wind, holding nothing for my happiness!

Through all my trials my Lord at my side, encouraging me on. Come on Kitty! Get up! You can do it! I'll bring you through! And who better than He to know, for He had created me! I had no choice but to hold on to Him, His word, and His love! See all along He knew what I was being fashioned for! I was being broken through all those years and tests, yet contained within all those pieces became a vessel of use, of God's so choosing and making. As it is with you as well!

He knows the finished product, for we are His choice!

As in, (Acts 9:13:16), as others looked on and said about God's choice in Paul, and maybe of me too! "Not them Lord, that's impossible". Yet God works with the impossible, with Him all things are possible, and He proves it through His people.

But the Lord said, "Go, for he (Paul), is an instrument whom I have chose to bring my name before Gentiles and Kings and before the people. I myself will show him how much he must suffer for the sake of my name". (Acts 9:15-16) For the sake of His name, not ours!

Never limit God, His ways nor His choices! For what man chooses, God does not! His ways are not our ways, and our ways are not His! Of which I am very grateful. For I too have no formal education! No Bible College behind me! No letter of recommendation! Nor Degrees!

Only the school of hard knocks, and of the Holy Spirit! They are my Teachers! For God's word says to study His word and show yourself approved! We must obey, following God, trusting Him and His hand upon our lives. He promises to bring us through our sufferings and hardships, not to spare us from them!

God had always chosen who we least expect, it is His way. That is how He proves Himself through the foolishness of mans thinking! We can do as we may! God does not need our stamp of approval of His choices in whom He wills to use! God does it over and over again! To prove this, that we are wrong and that He is right!

For God's foolishness is wiser than human wisdom, and God's weakness is stronger than human strength. For God chose what is foolish in the world to shame the wise; God chose what is weak in the world to shame the strong; God chose what is low and despised in the world, things that are not, to reduce to nothing things that are, so that no one might boast in the presence of God. He is the source of your life in Christ Jesus, who became for us the wisdom from God, and righteousness and sanctification and redemption, in order that, as it is written, let the one who boasts, boast in the Lord." (1 Corinthians 1:24-30)

The foolish that simply put their trust in Him, are the ones He chooses, again it is all about Him and nothing about us! All in what He did, nothing in us or what we could do. It is "He", the creator of the Universe and of you and I, that is the center of who we are, that is all that matters. It is only "He", love that will last, nothing else. Our over flowing love is the natural response to forgiveness and the consequence of our faith. But only we who realize this, the depth of our sin can appreciate the complete forgiveness God offers to us.

As the woman in (Luke 7:37-50), she is the example of love poured out, and what God desires from us, complete submission no matter who is looking on, to remain at the feet of Christ. To bathe His feet with our tears of love and repentance, anointing them with the precious contents held within us broken vessels. To be broken in order that we might be as Christ, to love, obey, submit to the will of the Father, as did Jesus.

"Let us love the Lord with all our hearts, and with all our souls, and with all our minds, and with all our strength. Let us love our neighbor as our self, there is no greater love than this." (Mark 12:30) It is simple, love God, love people!

May this love rule our thoughts, our decisions, our actions, our words, as we prepare to enter this "Promised Land". It is ours church, let us not grumble and complain, nor not believe God's word to us, let us enter in faith. True obedience comes from the heart, our motives should always be led by us asking ourselves this question. If this were Jesus standing before me would I be treating "Him", as I am treating this person? If not we need to move on church!

You remember the "Golden Rule"? In everything do to others as you would have them do to you! It is what Jesus taught as He walked this Earth, and now what we must live as we walk this earth!

"Jesus"
"God's Righteousness"

Then I heard what seemed to be the voice of a great multitude, like the sound of many waters and like the sound of mighty thunderpeals, crying out……

"Hallelujah!
For the Lord our God
the Almighty reigns.
Let us rejoice and exalt
and give Him glory,
for the marriage of the Lamb has come
and His bride has made herself ready;
to her it has been granted to be clothed
with fine linen, bright and pure,
for the linen is the righteous deeds of the saints." (Revelation 19:6-8)

Read this carefully church! For the bride "has made", herself ready! Are we making ourselves ready? Read it again, down a little further, she is clothed with fine linen. Bright and pure, and the linen, what is it that we are wearing? What is this linen? It is the righteous deeds of the saints.

Church it's time we woke up! Not to be caught without oil in our lamps, we must be ready! (Revelation 19:13-14), states "He is clothed in a robe dipped in blood, and His name is called, "THE WORD OF GOD", and the armies of heaven wearing fine linen, white and pure, were following Him on white horses. From His mouth comes a sharp sword with which to strike down the nations, and He will rule them with a rod of iron; He will tread the winepress of the fury of wrath of God the Almighty.

On His robe and on His thigh He has a name inscribed, "Kings of Kings and Lord of Lords." (Revelation 19:13-16)

Lets read this too very carefully church, not everyone is in here, only those wearing the fine linen, white and pure were following Him, "Jesus", on horses.

One must be wearing fine linen, what is this linen in the prior scripture? The fine linen we are to wear is the "righteous deeds of the saints", we are these saints! The fine linen is the righteous deeds of the saints. We are to be wearing "Him", Jesus! He alone is our righteousness, it is in Him alone that we make it, it is not in anything of ourselves. We could never be good enough, it is in His goodness that we stand here. It is our faith in Christ that brings us to that place of Awe! To God our heavenly Father! Christ alone is this bridge to God!

What are these righteous deeds? The work of Christ to save us! Not religious works on our part! "Hallelujah"! Amen!

The ultimate victory is that of Jesus, the work of what He did on the cross. See church, even God wanted to be back together with us. It is in what he did through His only Son that brings us there, he like us never wanted to be alone. It is this love of His giving that brings us to Him, and Him to us, Jesus! We could never be able to get to God on our own, it is only through His perfect sacrifice on the cross, His shedding His blood, that brings us back together. In Jesus, we are made perfect, not in ourselves, we do and always will fail God. He knew this! That is why we have Jesus, to allow fellowship again, now restored in and through the blood of Him coming and dying in our place. The price paid for all our sins that kept and remain to keep us separated from our Father, only through Jesus do you and I have reconciliation with our Father! If we believe, it is by faith that we enter!

We should be so humbly grateful to Him for this, His death so that we might have life, everlasting! We could be without sin, as we so think it. But just to be is not, enough. To say we have no sin, makes us liars. For God says all have sinned and have fallen short of His glory! We are sinners! Totally separated with the cross of Calvary bringing restoration to all. For to say we have no sin, is a sin! For it too against God's word, for He says we all have sinned. And He cannot lie!

“Jesus”
“God’s Salvation”

Are we ready to wear the linen as we prepare to mount the horses that await us church? His name is the “Word of God”! And the word became flesh and dwelt among us. See how important the “Word”, is church, it brought life to Christ as well to us. He is the spoken word as well as the word of God, in flesh as a man when He was here, as well as in Spirit now. God will never leave us, it is He alone that will bring us through. He carries us in, In Christ!

Christ’s first coming was that of forgiveness, yet this one, the final one will be that of judgement! Let us not be ashamed on that day church! Let us be ready in all the glory and splendor of who He is, and what He did for us! It is not us! Never has been and never will be. It is in He alone, it is all contained in and on the cross! The Will of the Father fulfilled in His Son Jesus, just so that you and I can come home!

Let us join together united in Christ Jesus, obey and be found worthy through the blood that was shed once, yet for all! The battle belongs to the Lord! He has already won! He will triumph church!

The Spirit and the Bride say come!
And let everyone who hears say, “Come”.
And let everyone who thirsts come.
Let anyone who wishes take the water of life as a gift!
(Revelation 22:17)

If you are reading this book and have never believed upon Christ and what He did for you in His dying on the cross. Jesus is that bridge back to God, our only way, the one and only way to everlasting life. His love for you and I in an action not in a mere word. We the Bride and the Spirit together say to you, “Come”. We extend an invitation to all the world to come to Jesus and experience the joys salvation brings. Salvation is not earned it is a freely given gift to us from Him, God our loving

Father who awaits us to come home to Him. Many are dying around us of thirst, reach out take of this living water, "Jesus", it is not too late. Drink of His love for you, never to thirst again. Everyone welcome, come drink!

From "Genesis to Revelation" all of it is about our relationship with Him, and He with us! Never doubt that! Trust Him and see when that final day comes if His word will prove true. You will not be disappointed, trust Him! His word will prove true! He is faithful to prove Himself to us!

We do not know the day or hour, but Jesus is coming back for us. This is good news to all whom put their trust in Him and believe He is who He says He is. Give your life to Him, surrender all for He is worthy! Worthy is the Lamb that sits upon the throne. We must not be caught off guard, for we only have this moment in time, we are never assured of tomorrow, it is today that He asks all to come!

"This God, His ways are perfect;
the promise of the Lord proves true;
He is a shield for all who take refuge "IN HIM".
(Psalm 18:30)

Won't you come to "Him", and let Him be your shield, He formed you, loves you, and wants you to come to Him and live forever in that place He has prepared for all His children. "Come"!

"For it's not by power, nor by might, but by my Spirit says the Lord of Hosts." This is in (Zechariah 4:6) shows us not to trust in our own strength, but to depend on God and the working of His Spirit!

Even in our coming to Him is by His might, for it is His drawing that pulls us to Him, for as we are drawn we can't help but fall to our very center of life.

The trials we face, also His to fight, it is not in us, or our strength but again contained in the working of God's Spirit. That is why we so need Him church, it is "He", that is our source of all.

Church it matters not what we have made of ourselves only what He has made of us. We do not mold ourselves or others, and should never, never put our hands to such a task. It is only God who can mold us and cause us no harm so that we might come out without spot or wrinkle.

Can we church lay down our lives, as did He? Can we go to the altar of sacrifice and die as He! Can we really count the cost of what we think others might think of us as we go! Are we ready?

Christ wasn't thinking of who was looking on when He laid it all down for us, as He hung there in the shame of His nakedness before man and God!

Can we now do the same? Can we come spiritually naked, and lay it all down and die to self before man and God? Can we?

For Christ was a man of no reputation, as we should be! But are we church of no reputation? Again it matters not what we make of ourselves only what He makes of us!

Let us quit dancing with the devil and fall into the arms of love that awaits us! With hands ready to mold us into thee image of His Son!

Leave your Sunday school classes, your pulpit, your guitar, your easy chair at home or your warmed pew at church! Come to the altar of sacrifice to the feet of Jesus! And lay it all down! Anoint His feet with your tears of repentance. It is time to die church of self!

We serve a mighty God, who awaits us! He awaits for us to come and be broken of all and remain at the feet of the one who saved us!

God will come in all His power and then be poured out from us onto all flesh so that He then might be made known.

We have a job to do church, let's get on with it! There is a hurting and dying world out there that needs Jesus!

They will not see Him if we stay safely tucked in between four walls!

Christ did not make a life for Himself, but He made a way of life for others!

He knew He must reveal the Father to all, and it was in dying to Himself that He did this, in obedience. As we must be willing to do now.

For in His death He gave us life, and now in our death we give Him life!

It is about time we prove who we serve and love in our actions that we take now, as He showed us His love with His actions upon the cross.

Our actions do speak louder than words, and it is this action that now needs to be revealed.

Let us speak with our hearts not our words, to die to self and prefer others before ourselves in the way that Christ did, as our example!

For we are not from here anyways, we are only passing through, there is a seat waiting for us in our true home, to the ones that believe and conquer, will sit there.

Do you believe? Do you? Will you conquer?

Let us prove it and go arm in arm to the altar of sacrifice as we are asked and lay it all down and die to ourselves. Let us be that living sacrifice as we are asked to be to a needy world.

Let us not stay in the seat of judgement as the men seated at the table with Jesus did, but be as the woman that came in love to the feet of Jesus to give her all, to be broken of all to receive His all.

We can do it church! We can do all things through Him that strengthens us, for the greater one that lives in us, is stronger than he that lives in the world.

All this here isn't about anything anyways without this, only one thing will remain, it is "Love". God is Love, therefore it is He that will remain…… LOVE!

You do not need to look up or reach out for Him, "just go within", He awaits you there church! Go to Him!

He knows who is reading this book at this moment, this too was in His plans, He knew all along those that will call upon Him, and those that are to come.

For God not only chose to come and dwell among us, yet to live within us as well! His life now ours! Our life now His!

"Jesus"
"God's Image"

See He knew you before Creation took place, He knew this day would come, He is our all and all, and all knowing!

He has waited so long for you to come to this place in your life, as you submit to His hand and are broken of all that is not of Him.

Know this too is in "His", plans as well as in "His Hands"!

We are crying out for Revival church! It begins with our breaking, for true Revival is the outpouring of the Holy Spirit! And He is contained within us. So for Him to be poured out, means we can no longer remain the same church! To stay like this makes us useless vessels, instead of useful vessels. We must now allow the breaking to begin, so that God can come forth in all the love and power that that He is. May we be obedient, submitting to "His Hand" as He begins this work so that His will can be done and His word may be fulfilled!

Let us surrender to His work in us! For it is His works that matters, not ours! Even our good is as a filthy rag to God. Our only good is again in Him! Jesus!

Of this gospel I have become a servant according to the gift of God's grace, that was given to me by the working of His power (Ephesians 3:7)

For to forget what lies behind and strain forward to what lies ahead! (Philipians 3:13)

There to submit to God, resisting the enemy and he will flee from me! (James 4:7)

Making me complete in every good work to do His will, working in us what is well pleasing in His sight, through Jesus Christ, to whom be the glory forever and ever. Amen! (Hebrews) 13:21)

To be known as a people who have been turning the world upside down. (Acts 17:6)

And I appeal to you therefore, brothers and sisters, by the mercies of God to present your bodies as a living sacrifice, holy and acceptable to God, which is our spiritual worship! (Romans 12:1)

For although He was a Son, he learned obedience through what He suffered; and having been made perfect, He became the source of eternal salvation for all who obey Him (Hebrews 5:8)

O come, let us bow down and worship,
let us kneel before the Lord, our Maker!
For He is our God,
and we are the people of His pasture,
and the sheep of His hand!
(Psalm 95:6-7)

For I have no greater goal in my life, than to devote my life, and my service to God. And may the Holy Spirit that abides within us continue on in His power bringing us through to the finish line. For our Father to say to us, "Well done my good and faithful servants, enter in!"

Let us go, and prepare to enter in church!

"He is the pearl of great price" (Matthew 13:45)

Come and take my hand, for I too go to be broken of all, to submit at the feet of Him that gave all for me, and now asks us to come and do as He, and now give our all to Him. It will cost us something, but then "He", is worth it! Amen!

Yes! Something of worth will always be costly!

Yet! He paid that costly price for us, such love contained in Him, who willingly went, and did the Fathers Will.

As we must too, now go willingly, to do the Fathers Will.

To there remain until "He", is finished molding us the church! Into the Image of His beloved Son. Who broke and gave all!

Let us go arm in arm!

He awaits us!

Shall we begin to enter in, together, united as one in the love of "Him"!

Let us now lay all down and obey! He is calling us to come!

For "Deep calls to Deep"!

LET US GO

For all things my hand has made,
and so all things are mine, says
the Lord. But this is the man to
whom I will look, he that is….
Humble and Contrite in Spirit,
and trembles at my word."

Isaiah 66:2

"POEMS"

"OH SAINTS OF GOD"

Oh Saints of God
Rise up the call has gone forth in
the land, do all in Christ Jesus
and then stand.
Oh Saints of God
Gird yourself with the word of God
it is the hour, be strong in the
Lord, in the strength of his power
Oh Saints of God
Get up out of your comfort zone, and
pray, the enemy is roaming about
this very day.
Oh Saints of God
Stand in the full "Armor of God",
raise up his shield and sword,
he will conquer the victory is in
our Lord.
Oh Saints of God
Don't go by sight or what you feel,
speak the word to the devil, for
he's out to rob, kill and steal.
Oh Saints of God
Quit getting angry at God, feeling
sorry for yourself and cry, get up
get up the "Blood", has been shed,
its time to die.
Oh Saints of God
Rise above your flesh, speak to it,
remind it, it is dead, and know
now in God, you are Spirit led.
Oh Saints of God
Arise God says, arise my children
and fight, the victory is won, cast
out fear, already triumphed and
done

Oh Saints of God
Run the course, claim your prize
at the end of the race, you will
then come and meet God, face to
face.
Oh Saints of God
Awards then given and a victory
wreath too put upon your head,
but all is given back to Jesus
for his Blood shed.
Oh Saints of God
Rise up in His power, the Holy
Spirit within, this is thee hour
Oh! Hallelujah Saints in Him we
win!

MY MASTER HAND

Fill me Lord and make me whole
Only you can satisfy my soul
Shaped by my Masters hand
Chosen to do your work upon this land
You have lifted the veil from my eyes
I no longer sit and listen to lies
The depth of your love more than I can take in
Yet I ask no questions only remove myself from sin
All you have done for me how could I want less
You have showed me the way through the darkness
Holding my hand each step of the way
Morning, noon, and night of each day
Lending me your ear, as I broke and gave all
You knew all along my life and its call
You put it there, all from the very start
Always drawing me close to your very heart
Your faithfulness, uncompared to a thing
Your love and praises forever will I sing
I will bless your holy name as my soul gives
Everything back unto you God, you are why I live

"OUR PURPOSE"

To the one who pleases God, He gives wisdom, knowledge and joy,
This is not a game in life, nor should we treat it as a toy.

Life is in whom! We know "God"! Not what we know as "Man"!
To walk by faith, and not questioning Him with wonders of if we can.

If not here for Gods use, will and joy, then what to you I ask?
For our only purpose is to serve and love, God, this is our only task.

Nothing else matters nor should stand in our way,
will we leave our mark for God or go as the world may?

For his ways, words and will to be held high,
going forth, united, to conquer, stand firm and occupy.

Of him will we ever listen, obey and learn?
Or will we stand ashamed upon our Lord's return?

"GENTLE-MAN"

I choose to be a living sacrifice, epistle of Christ, written with the Spirit of the living God, without depth nor measure,

I love to do the will of God, because God works in me to will and do His good pleasure.

My life now in the Spirit is far above the material life as the heavens are above the earth as seen,

My breath now yours, my life in your hands, for this is of you, my life is yours to deem.

All done and known to your delight and cause, your salvation for all, your truths in us will ring,

Revealing to me the preciousness and power of the blood of Christ, the King.

Of this you stand in truth, honor and love and do declare,

To do this day, no longer veiled and dead, but by your Spirit made aware.

Praise and glory and all honor are on my lips daily, offered in my trial,

In the fire of life by your hand, polished and finely smoothed by your file.

To come forth as precious gold of great worth and of beauty uncompared now,

But amidst it Lord, I questioned your hand, and asked Oh! but how.

No longer I yield to the way of death, for I now say how far, oh yes I can,

For you my source, substance and call, you have reached down and brought me out, you my GENTLEMAN.

BY YOUR FATHERS SIDE

All were present that day and knew who you were
The sun, moon, and stars didn't even stir
On that day of triumph when the Son did rise
All of creation stood still looking into your eyes
The tree limbs bent low, the clouds parted
Oceans didn't rise, nor was the morning ever started
The earth trembled beneath the mountains high
Flowers were being crushed and gave a great sigh
The cross lay bear that once you were upon
But death can't hold you, for from it you are gone
Now seated in the Heavenlies by your Fathers side
You are restored now to your rightful place and our guide
The glory of your name shall live forever more
Your word now eternally proclaimed from shore to shore

"ALONE AM I"

There I sat and did cry,
Alone I was, alone was I.

Shed forth tears to thee,
Crying out Oh God can you see?

The tears falling, staining my face,
You came in silence stating your case.

Yes, I see and hear and do care,
This of me you receive, this cause we share.

You Lord? You Lord? I did not know!
Like you again held tight to not show.

Your tears mine, shed and tossed?
Held and counted all of no loss.

Yes! You alone my child, you like I,
As I Am in a state of why.

In my image you were cast,
Together we will conquer, this not to last.

Alone here like you, call and wait,
Where, oh where is my mate?

Oh Lord! In shame I now sit
My tears wiped dry, your light is lit.

Let me not cry in want a more,
Only sit before you the way the door.

Forgive myself of there I sat,
I of this wipe my feet on this mat.

No more to murmur and complain of mine own,
Set aside now for you Lord are my life, you are
Like I alone.

Alone together are we, alone to each other are we,
Only unto this one thing I beseech thee.

Await me Lord, await I do come,
I will be thine, and you will be mine.

I as you will await, together are we,
Our love alone no longer to be.

No longer will we ever be alone, to this we did die,
Forgive me Lord, For you were alone as I.

"CHOSEN"

As I sat amidst my trials of life,
Only constant pain held me amongst the
Over whelming strife.

My eyes filled with hopelessness of tears,
As waves of such formed my face for years.

Not to find a one the same as I,
Day in and day out against this pain I did cry.

My arms held tightly by my side,
For this pain knew there was no one along to guide.

A whisper one day did I hear,
You must come closer for I am near.

The whisper that day did I hear, saying no more alone
are you to be left on the shelf,
For you my daughter I have chosen for myself.

Come now and let me surround you with my life,
You my child are to be my bride my wife.

I have taken you, adorned you with such trials bringing
you to me and me alone,
This love of me is precious and to you I have been shown.

"THORNS IN MY BROW"

The color red, the taste bitter, the feel of
warmth as it runs down my face,

As I hung in the shame of my nakedness, yet
not a word to plead my case.

Inside broken, a pain to great to compare,
outside my skin did there tear,

The filth of the world laid upon me that day,
I took it all I took it to bear.

Eyes wide open to see into the faces of all,
My heart for you and in this was my call.

Long ago I kept this within,
Yet unseen now, but then I seen you in all your sin.

Before you came here to this earth and did live,
I foreknew you, made you and said of this I give.

Of no question did I ask, of or how,
Only for you I took, THORNS IN MY BROW.

LORD OF HOSTS

There is nothing impossible for you, oh God, my Lord, Savior
and King of thee I praise, worship, bow down and sing

I delight to do thy will, oh God, my love, hope, strength, and shield everything a failure, except that of your Spirit, of this do I cry out and do yield.

Called to be a living sacrifice and to die
Yet unburied at times I remain alive, sinning and ask why?

You come in all your splendor and glory and of this say the most

Daughter it is not by might nor by power,
But by my spirit, says the Lord of hosts.

PLACE OF AWE

My heart is yours and yours is mine

Our love to last throughout time

You use the simple to confound the wise

I know I’m nothing in mans eyes

But you God proved me of worth

And that’s all that matters to me on earth

Once we are together in that place of awe

Love will be the only reigning law

WOUNDED YET NOT SLAIN

I've been wounded in this life yet not slain

Many have tried to kill me and brought pain

Yet unable for my spirit won't be possessed nor taken

No acclaim to myself nor to man I am not shaken

Neither corruption comes near nor mans rule

For within me no matter what I am ready for a duel

This life worthless and of no cost

Never to turn back and forever be lost

For my God is forever showing me my call

Leading me on to receive his all

Urging me on each step of the way

Reassuring me it will all be worth it someday

I smile therefore and now press on

Knowing all is behind me and forever now gone

BEHOLD THE LAMB

The day they rolled away the stone

Some thought you to be alone

Yet we know angels were in view

Comforting you and bringing you through

For hidden in you was the great treasure

The Holy Spirits power without measure

You put our names in the Lambs Book of Life

Waiting for your Spirit to be revealed in us your wife

The thorns now removed and a crown there now reigns

For it was all for the Fathers glory, his word ordains

Behold the Lamb of God, the Man Christ Jesus

Forsaken, killed, betrayed, yet our friend who will never leave us

SWEET SURRENDER

I'm possessed by your Spirit I must confess

Leaving nothing for myself, I want you and nothing less

Past pleasures behind me, and now to flee

I live no more, it is your life that lives in me

Your love, grace and mercy so faithful and divine

All for me to partake of, freely all is mine

Healed by your living waters that flow from within

Once I was held by the worlds death and all its sin

For in it all, you shielded me, you my Great Defender

And all you wanted from me was my sweet surrender

"SECRET PLACE"

Sweet breath of God, come let your presence be known,
Here awaits all glory, power and honor are yours alone.

Steadfast I obey you and no matter what I will stand,
With my eyes fixed on you and your outstretched hand.

Your beauty Lord all set in the perfect brilliance of your face,
I will not wonder away, I remain hid in that secret place.

Not to be called out by others nor disturbed by a word,
Only remain hid in you, no other have I heard.

For I know the weak ban together to pull down the strong,
But you God are righteous, standing for truth, they are wrong.

You come Father and set your ways before me your child,
Let me not be led astray by others and all their wilds.

It is in you I now rest, you alone my love to pursue and chase,
I will not sway, I will stand firm hid in you, my secret place.

MY DWELLING PLACE

Oh my love, my center, desire and need

Only to your call I answer, your step to lead

At thy feet I sit, and now do remain

For life I've tasted, it holds nothing for my gain

While in that life I once did try and live

But you assured me it had nothing to give

And there once I pondered on this dreadful thought

You have loved me and proven you have not forgot

I know my love, rather in word, thought or deed, is not of me

There too I am at a loss and only receive of thee

I, nothing on my own, nor of myself have to give

Now I rejoice, remain in you and now I truly live

Even when you put me in the fire

My love for you only grew, strengthening my desire

I will not go from your side nor your sight

You have kept me protected in all your might

You my very flow of living water, life and grace

My purpose is in you my Lord, for you are my dwelling place

“MY SUBSTANCE”

You God stir my emotions in my soul to go on,
Yet of lost loves around me now are gone.

You God call me daily to remain at your side,
As a child I come in wonderous eyes opened wide.

You God made me to sit and lay, my feet to walk,
My breath to breathe, my eyes to see, my mouth to talk.

You God call the wind to stir and become quiet in you,
My heart beats, my eyes blink, I am totally in you to do.

You God my mind is there to capture and remember all,
My hand that writes and knows even its call.

You God set in motion all of your substance let it be known,
To feel the warmth of your presence in all this you are shown.

You God “MY SUBSTANCE”, and shield,
To you God I submit and do yield.

“BACK HOME”

Asking of us to come, just come sit and
receive from above,

Such grace, mercy and compassion, it is
yours, His love.

Deep within we hear you say, no one else
I am the way,

Our spirits bear witness and beckon come
near, oh come this day.

We answer and say “yes Lord”, we come, we
are here and do hear you voice,

Knowing all these years you have wanted
us to make this choice.

Calling us “BACK HOME”, where we belong,

Whispers so sweetly they sing as an ever
beautiful song.

Your words gently put upon our hearts,

There since beginning never to part.

Come home my children, come to your
Father of birth,

Come unto me to a place prepared not of
this earth.

Turned to gold through your trials of
fire,

Picked up out of the great filth and
mire.

Come “BACK HOME”, the table is set,

Everything in place all needs here are
met.

"YOU ALONE I ADORE"

Choice of angels and of man, both rejected you
and of no good,
But you oh God, only want love, you oh God
are not understood.

My heart does cry within so deep of this beguile,
But deep within I must depart from this and deep
within I smile.

Smile Lord; for ever present there you are in my
sight,
Dawning constantly bringing forth in me thy
eternal light.

While others look upon me and stand to judge,
they dare,
Lest I stay at your side and in your arms safe
from a care.

Safely there I remain safe from the enemies lure,
To your bosom I am held in you Lord,
"YOU ALONE I ADORE".

“OH BUT DUST”

Formed from the dust of the ground, you breathed into our
nostrils the breath of life, without a sound.
Silently there we lay, a non living thing, then you oh God
spoke, and with an ever constant beat our heart there awoke.
Lord may we ever know your love in this matter the same,
yet never let our life bring to you shame.
Oh breath of life, eternally known and cause of me,
let me be pleasing to you alone, my eyes gaze set upon thee.
Set me apart, consecrated in Christ Jesus, your love,
to remind me daily of your choice from high above.
You Oh Lord, down from your throne you came and died,
bringing me to your light, open and available not to hide.
Love, pure and divine, hold me ever so tightly so close,
and know Lord it is you, only you, I love the most.

“DESTINED TO DIE”

Before creation took place or ever thought of man-
You God stood silent, loved us and wanted a land-
In your presence there to stand still, thought deep within-
Once I do this I know there will be sin-
Man left alone, deadly in deeds and words would fall-
But, God knew this and said upon me they will call-
Yet alone as alone could be, alone though alone you were-
Of this you stated and said, I will do, of this I am sure-
Deep within held close to your heart, there you cared-
And, said of this I am not alone, my love is to be shared-
Of myself I give, my love my only begotten son-
He is your way, on Calvary to all death, He has won-
Just receive of me and not ask why, for I was
“DESTINED TO DIE”

HOLY LOVE

Holy love - Holy love, I know you see my heart
Holy love - Holy love, hold me close to never part
Melt me down cast the mold
In the fire you do there hold
No more spots nor wrinkles show
I'm held captive and you know
Holy love - Holy love, I now can see your face
Holy love - Holy-love, forever I shall feel your embrace
Melt me down cast the mold
In the fire you do there hold
No more spots nor wrinkles show
I'm held captive and you know
Holy love - Holy love, you are here when I cry and weep
Holy love - Holy love, and each tear you do there keep
Melt me down cast the mold
In the fire you do there hold
No more spots nor wrinkles show
I'm held captive and you know
Holy love - Holy love, only this one thing I do beseech
Holy love - Holy love, keep me safe within your reach
Melt me down cast the mold
In the fire you do there hold
No more spots nor wrinkles show
I'm held captive and you know
Holy love - Holy love
I'm held captive and you know

"ON WINGS OF LOVE"

Brushing my face with touch of no sight;
In tenderness unknown but of great might.

Down you come to my cheek and there do say;
Reach out up above, no care but me, I am the way.

In a flight you leave, as if to me you tease;
I call, wait, Oh Precious One, stay do not leave.

I await, await again for your touch;
I have longed for in myself so much.

Only your love does so gently come unto me;
I look to no other, only unto thee.

Crying out to you, bring yourself back to me, on wings;
Where angels do praise and thusly sings.

Come again to my side;
It is your presence I await, to myself I have died.

To this self set aside to no longer yield;
You my salvation my cause my shield.

Come here again I long for your touch;
Without seeing you oh Lord, I love you so much.

On wings come I do await and be still;
For of myself you put aside and did kill.

You my lover of distance, yet closer than my own skin;
With threads of love you healed me you did mend.

Take me with you on your wings high above;
From you yet unseen I have received great love.

Let me go with you, lover of my soul;
It is with you alone I am made whole.

Do not leave me once you go I pray;
I press my cheek to you and do say.

Come and whisper once more;
Of your love and nothing else am I sure.

Come my love from high above;
Take me on your wings of love.

To a place far away from here your eternal light does shine;
Away, far away to a place outside of time.

High above, oh high above on wings of love;
Oh high above on your wings of love.

I am yours my Father, I am yours and you are mine;
Ever we are eternally entwined.

"LIVING SACRIFICE"

Peace alone comes from God, and only in
knowing Him,
Joys to receive and love from within.

Submit all you hold inside,
he awaits you with open arms to guide.

Nothing held secret, all is layed bare,
but he is a true friend, of them he'll not share.

Give him your all, he awaits you this day,
for of his life he gave and down he did there lay.

Only to in turn give back unto you,
life everlasting, and for you to come through.

To now lay down there your life,
to give as he, and be a living sacrifice.

POWER OF PENTECOST

Oh Precious Father send your Holy Ghost power,
Prepare us Father as we wait for thee hour.
Send your fire upon us the church,
Let us remain before you and search.
Give us your children flames about our head,
For we have no power and are dead.
We will tarry until endowed from on high,
Receiving power from the Holy Ghost you cannot lie.
Send forth your Spirit to us for we are in shame,
Lacking all you have for us, power and tongues of flame.
We need your power to heal, set free the captive and forgive,
For it is only in you we now breathe, move and now live.
For it is not by power, nor by might, but by your Spirit, Lord,
We must be in unity, always submit and be in one accord.
We need your Spirit, Lord to raise the dead and heal the lame,
We only want to prove to all and above all proclaim your name.
Send down your rain and Shekina glory in this place,
Fill this house with rushing wind and your shining face.
Your presence alone is needed here so much,
We need you Lord we so need your touch.
Only you will do and no one else do we depend upon,
Rather it be midnight or in the early morning dawn.
We are here seeking your face, your power, your hand,
We will repent, turn from our ways so you can heal our land.

POWER OF PENTECOST

Oh so sorry are we Lord, we do admit our wrong.

We've all wasted time, been comfortable for way to long.

Yet we are here and still await your anointing and zeal,

For you have set before us a feast, a banquet meal.

The world needs you God, trust us once again with your heart,

We will serve you, have faith, love you, to never again part.

Oh Precious Father, send us your power of Pentecost,

For if we stay like this we will surely be lost.

So now we open up before you and give you our all this very hour,

Oh God we do so plead, send us your Holy Ghost power.

"…He humbled Himself
and became obedient to death-
even death on a cross!
Therefore God exalted Him
to the highest place
and gave Him the name
that is above every name."

[Philippians 2:8-9]

"Jesus"!

"Instrument of Peace"

Lord make me an instrument of your peace, where there is hatred let me so love, where there is injury, pardon, and where there is doubting let me bring your faith.

Lord make me an instrument of your peace, where there is despairing let me bring your hope, where there is darkness your light, and where there is sadness let me bring your joy.

Only my Master, grant that I might seek, not so much to be consoled as to console, to be understood as to understand, not so much to be loved as to love another.

For it is in giving that we now receive, it is pardoning that we are now pardoned. It is in dying that we are born again.

And Lord make me an instrument of your peace, where there is hatred let me bring your love........ By.. St. Francis Assisi

Let this be a prayer of our heart and our life. May God bless you, and may you be found at peace upon his return, in his love shed for us all, may we be found complete lacking in nothing. He is always with you, always for you and has waited for you, his beloved children.

Come home! He awaits you with open arms of Love.
The Lord bless you and keep you;
the Lord make his face to shine upon you,
and be gracious to you;
the Lord lift up his countenance upon you;
and give you peace....[Numbers 7:22-27]

For this is His Land and we are His People!
And this is the time to rebuild His Temple
of Praise!

About the Author

Through my testimony and strong faith in the Lord, I hope and desire to see people walk through circumstances and arise in faith. Knowing that any hardship and suffering that we experience is united with Christ.

Through faith I remain a simple instrument of use, a vessel unto His call, having no other purpose or plan except to grow in this life that He has called me into. I am no one special, not a world traveler or lecturer, no formal education, just a simple love for the Lord.

I wish to encourage others in similar situations to cleave to the Lord, to realize He is unchanging, ever present and to respond to the truth in the Scriptures.